# IMPROV QUILTS

# IMPROV QUILTS

## BUILDING CONFIDENCE IN COLOR AND TECHNIQUE

**LAURA LOEWEN**

SEARCH PRESS

First published in 2025
Search Press Limited
Wellwood, North Farm Road,
Tunbridge Wells, Kent TN2 3DR


Printed in China.

ISBN: 978-1-80092-172-6
ebook ISBN: 978-1-80093-152-7



**Publishers' note**
All the step-by-step photographs in this book feature the author, demonstrating quilting techniques. No models have been used.

**Suppliers**
If you have difficulty in obtaining any of the materials and equipment mentioned in this book, then please visit the Search Press website for details of suppliers: www.searchpress.com

**Bookmarked Hub**
Copies of the coloring sheets are also available to download free from the Bookmarked Hub: www.bookmarkedhub.com

The projects in this book have been made using imperial measurements, and the metric equivalents provided have been calculated following standard conversion practices. The imperial measurements are often rounded to the nearest 0.5cm for ease of use except in rare circumstances; however, if you need more exact measurements, there are a number of excellent online converters that you can use. Always use either metric or imperial measurements, not a combination of both.

ABOUT THE AUTHOR
To see more of the author's work, visit:
www.quiltfortcompany.com
Instagram: @quiltfortco

# Table of CONTENTS

# Introduction

When I first came to improvisational design after almost 20 years of quilting, I wasn't sure how I felt about this uncertain formula but I was ready to try something new. I decided to stay in my comfort zone and simply improv-piece some traditional designs of quilt blocks. For these initial experiments I used a ruler to cut, and played around with color and prints. Admittedly, I was reluctant because I am a self-proclaimed perfectionist. What about the corners that won't match? How will my project stay organized if everything is willy-nilly? The instant I finished my first block, however, I fell in love with the imperfections of improv.

I was hooked from that moment on. I have since gone on to make and teach ruler-cut and ruler-free improv piecing, and improv appliqué. I have worked with my favorite traditional blocks to create improv quilts and have created original compositions. All the while, I have also been experimenting with color and creating gradient and flow in my work.

I am often asked how I choose colors for my quilts and how I approach improv quilting. Many makers who ask for guidance are new to the improv process or want to improve their color selection and placement. Whether you are an experienced quilter new to improv, or have tried out improv quilting in the past but want to master it, this book will provide a guided approach to help you gain the confidence you need to create your own original improv quilts.

"... the qualifier for improv is not knowing the result before you begin."

# WHAT IS IMPROV QUILTING?

There are many ways to define improv quilting. For me, the qualifier for improv is not knowing the result before you begin. However, there are two more parts to my answer.

The first is about technique. What part of your design are you going to improv? The color, shapes, cutting, or piecing can all be a sole improv component to your design. Or you can combine these for a more complex composition. Each ingredient requires a specific skill, and you will learn to be confident in developing and integrating those skills.

The second is the approach you take at the beginning of your project. Even though you don't know what the result will look like, you can still have an idea of where your work will go. To me, improv does not mean not having a plan. It just means having an open-ended plan that can change as you create. You can start with just a concept and make decisions organically – making and designing at the same time, or you can stick within the boundaries of a traditional quilt block but be freer and more creative with your cutting and piecing. This can be applied to any of the components mentioned above.

# HOW TO USE THIS BOOK

I've written this book to be read from beginning to end, and for the projects to be worked through in the order presented in the book to develop your improv quilting and color confidence. However, feel free to jump around and play with the different techniques described in the earlier chapters of the book in any order before you move on to the later chapters on advanced improv and how to design from a blank slate.

If you choose to work on the projects in order, they will build upon each other, adding new skills and techniques as you go. I take this approach to provide you with baby steps before I ask you to design your own original improv quilt. That way you can build up your confidence before being thrown in front of a blank design wall. There is no reason to feel panic and terror at the prospect of making an improv quilt. Improv quilting should be fun and relaxing.

I know improv quilting can be intimidating, and color selection can be daunting. It might seem a bit basic to start at the beginning again if you have been a quilter for a while, but taking a step back and building your eye for color really is the best place to begin. After getting comfortable with how color selection and placement can affect your quilt design, you will look at traditional blocks—a comfort zone for many quilters—to learn ruler-cut and ruler-free improv piecing techniques. When you have built your confidence in those skills, you can move into advanced improv with curved piecing. By the time you reach the end of the book you will have learned to begin to rely on your instincts and take on your projects without fear.

This book provides detailed descriptions of the skills you will use for improv quilting and, where relevant, includes measurements like a quilt pattern. It is not my intention for you to make exact replicas of the sample quilts, but to develop your own improv skills so you can use them to create unique quilts. My hope is that you can work through the projects in this book and gain the confidence to be the improv quilter you want to be.

# Tools and materials

Simply put, you only need fabric, scissors, needle, and thread to sew an improv quilt. However, there are many other tools and materials that you may want to take advantage of to make the process easier and possibly more enjoyable.

## DESIGNING

**Pens and colored pencils (1)**
It is beneficial to have coloring and drawing tools on hand when working through your project color story.

**Work surface**
A large work surface will give you a place to arrange fabrics and lay out components before moving them to a design wall. I recommend a 24 x 36in (61 x 91.5cm) or 30 x 48in (76 x 122cm) surface, in addition to a table for your sewing machine.

**Design wall**
A design wall is a key player in improv work. Being able to arrange fabrics and move pieces around before sewing them is an integral part of learning to create your design organically. A piece of batting tacked to a wall works well to easily rearrange pieces. If you don't have a dedicated sewing space or an empty wall available, you can spread batting out on the floor or a large table. To store away between work sessions, roll up the batting, keeping the pieces in place.

**Tape measure (2)**
A 60in (152.5cm) soft tape measure is a useful tool for measuring large segments while working on improv quilts. I have found keeping a 12ft (3.6m) retractable carpenter's tape measure in my sewing kit is helpful, too.

**Fabric**
I highly recommend designer-quality quilting cotton in solid colors and/or prints. However, I also never hesitate to incorporate cotton woven fabrics, shot cottons, and linen blends into my improv projects. If fabric yardage is not available to you, or if you are looking for a more sustainable quilting practice, you can use any light or medium weight 100 percent cotton, or a cotton-linen blend fabric.

## CUTTING

**Rotary cutter (3)**
My 45mm rotary cutter is one of my most-used tools during my improv projects. Make sure you start with a sharp blade and change it frequently to maintain a safe cutting experience. I also keep a 28mm rotary cutter in my sewing kit for detailed or smaller cuts.

**Cutting mat (4)**
Using a self-healing mat when cutting with a rotary cutter and as a work surface is good practice. I recommend a mat with measurement markings in inches or centimeters. With improv work I am comfortable switching between measuring with my rulers and measuring with the markings on my cutting mat. Use the largest cutting mat you can fit on your work surface. I prefer 24 x 36in (61 x 91.5cm), but you could also use 18 x 24in (45.5 x 61cm).

**Rulers (5)**
I use a ruler as a straight edge to cut against for ruler-cut improv quilting. My favorites are 6 x 24in (15 x 61cm), 4 x 14in (10 x 35.5cm), 3½ x 3½in (9 x 9cm), and 8½ x 8½in (21.5 x 21.5cm) quilting rulers. I also use these to measure or estimate lengths. I use the corner of a quilting ruler or a T-square to make 90-degree corners. A long spirit level or laser level can also be useful for ensuring a straight edge when finishing your quilts. You may see ruler, quilting ruler, and straightedge used interchangeably, but essentially all mean a straight edge to cut against.

**Scissors/snips (6)**
I keep both fabric and paper scissors within arm's reach in my sewing space, as there are instances when I need to use both types of scissors. In addition, I keep a pair of small snips next to my sewing machine for easy access.

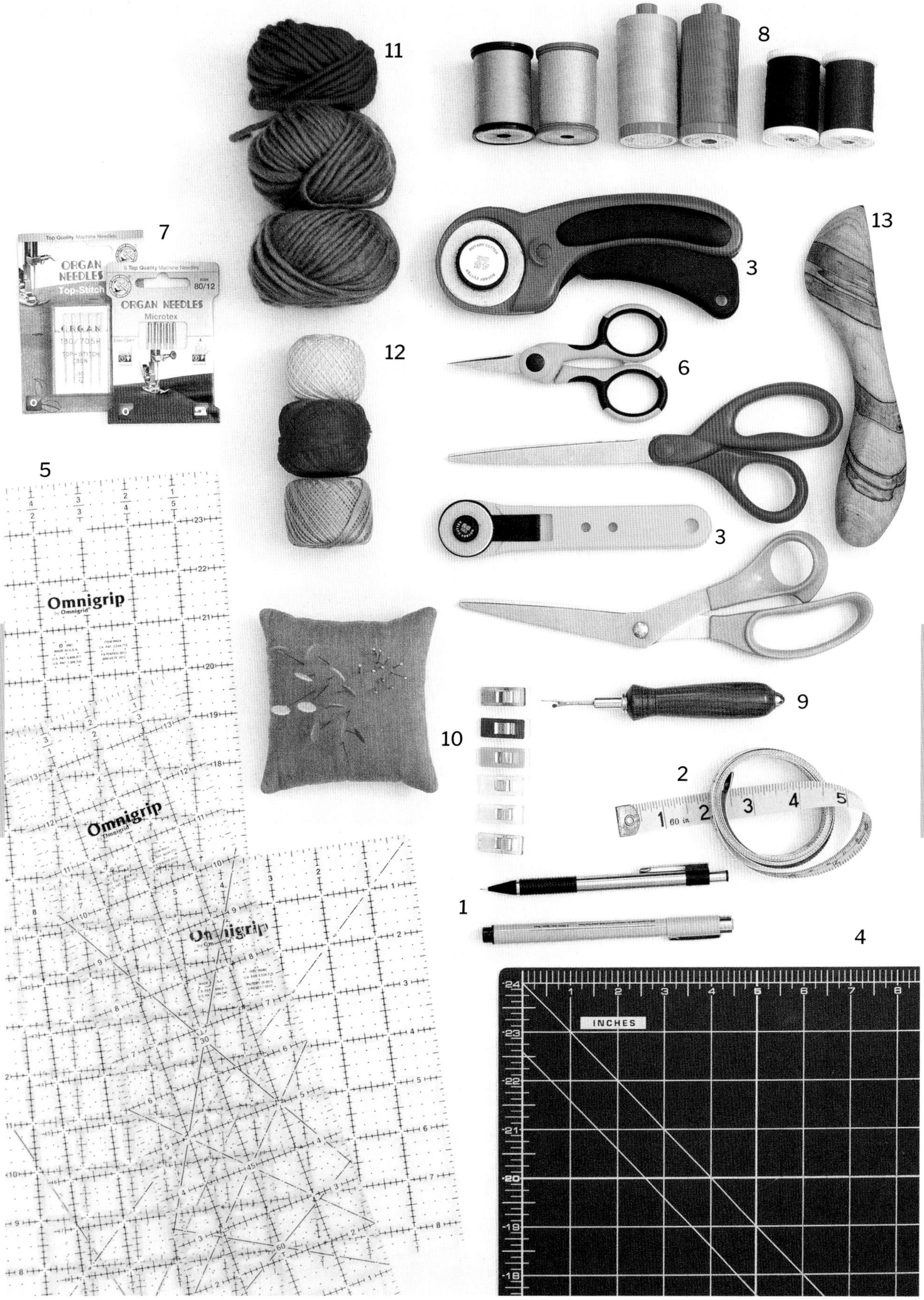

11
8
7
13
3
12
6
5
3
9
10
2
1
4

## ASSEMBLY AND SEWING

**Sewing machine and needles (7)**
A basic sewing machine with a straight stitch is all you need. I like to use Microtex: 70/10 needles for piecing and 90/14 needles for quilting (top-stitching).

**Thread (machine) (8)**
For piecing I like a 50 weight, 100 percent cotton, high-quality thread. There is a wide variety of threads you can choose from for quilting. I have used anything from the same 50 weight, 100 percent cotton thread I use for piecing, or 40 weight cotton, to silk, polyester, and even 12 weight cotton in my machine.

**Seam ripper (9)**
It's always good to have a seam ripper on hand.

**Iron and board**
A good hot and steamy iron with a nicely sized ironing board works well for almost any quilt project. Alternatively, keep a spray bottle of water near your iron to create steam without putting water through the iron. I also like to use a wool pressing mat.

**Pins and clips (10)**
A variety of pin options can be used for different parts of improv quilting. I keep safety pins, 1¼in (3cm) dressmaker/tailor straight pins, and 2in (5cm) flat-head straight pins in my sewing kit for use in my projects. Clips are a good alternative to pins.

## FINISHING

**Batting (also known as wadding)**
There are many types and weights of batting to choose from. My preference is lightweight, 100 percent cotton or a cotton–bamboo blend. However, if you want a quilt with more bulk, weight, or fluffiness, you can look at polyester, wool, or other high-loft batting types.

**Wool yarn (11)**
If you are going to tie your quilt (see page 119), I recommend wool yarn. Wool is a very durable and secure option for quilt tying. It will felt itself and become more secure over time.

**Perle cotton (12)**
For hand quilting, my preference is perle cotton size 8. There are other weights that work well including size 5 and size 12.

**Hera marker (13)**
You can mark quilting lines in several ways. I prefer to use a Hera marker that creates a crease in the quilt top.

## *My workspace*

I'm lucky to have a dedicated sewing space in my home. My walls are white, bright, and clean. I hang a few inspirational framed pieces of art on my walls, but most of my wall space is occupied by a large design wall, about 9ft (2.7m) long and 7ft (2.1m) high. A bookshelf houses workshop supplies and samples, thread, and my scrap-fabric bins. My fabric stash is stored in small bins under my cutting table, sorted by type: blenders; novelties and text; low-volume prints; rare or hard-to-find designers I love; a particular designer group; mixed solids, linen, and woven fabrics; and large cuts for backings or background yardage. Each bin is then organized in color order. I have two work surfaces, my sewing table and my cutting table, which also acts as my computer desk.

There is a small closet in the space that houses storage for my show quilts, miscellaneous supplies such as ribbon, notions, felt, batting, shipping supplies, and photography equipment.

# Quilting basics

You are probably reading this book because you are ready to take the next step in your quilting journey. There's no need to change your ways when it comes to basic skills and tasks. However, if you're open to trying a different method, you may find a new way that works better for improv quilting.

## Seam allowance

As with traditional quilt piecing, I use a ¼in (5mm) seam allowance for all my improv piecing. However, there is typically no reason to have a precise scant ¼in (5mm) seam allowance. I often prefer a generous ¼in (6–7mm), especially for ruler-free or curved piecing.

## Pressing direction

Pressing direction is a very personal preference. I like to press open 99 percent of the time. The reasons I press open are: 1) I never quilt in the ditch to finish a project, and 2) I find that my blocks lay flattest pressed open when I am sewing on the bias for improv piecing. However, you may be comfortable pressing to the side, and I am not here to change your ways—I do press to the side on occasion. I encourage you to try both options and then make your decision.

## Pinning

Again, this is a personal choice. Most of the time I do not use pins because there is a lot of wiggle room in improv quilting to accommodate imperfections. There are times when I do like to use pins, mostly on large curves, but you may find that using clips or glue better suits your sewing style.

LETTERPRESS

# TIPS AND TRICKS: IMPROVE YOUR IMPROV

## Using measuring tools

Just because you are creating an improv quilt doesn't mean you can never use your cutting mat or ruler to measure or align pieces when cutting and piecing.

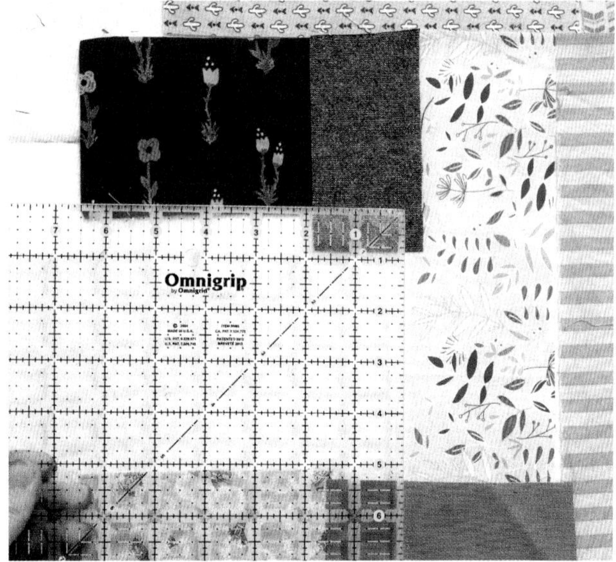


Use a ruler or tape to measure spaces where you will add pieces. Add ½in (1cm) when cutting to allow for seams. For the space shown, I would cut a 7½ x 6in (19 x 15cm) piece.

For ruler-free cutting you can use your cutting-mat lines to estimate the size of your cut piece. Here I have cut freehand an approximately 5 x 4in (13 x 10cm) piece.

## Filler

Sometimes you will want to attach two pieces together that are not of the same size. You will want to add fabric to the smaller piece to make it big enough to attach to the larger piece. I call this "filler." You are filling in the space—patching to change the size—on one improv segment to make it so that you do not have to cut a significant amount off the next segment.

A rule-of-thumb I like to use is: if the difference is greater than ½in (1cm), add a filler piece instead of cutting down the larger section to accommodate the smaller one.

When adding filler, first align the edges of the two pieces/sections you are working with. Measure the heights and find the difference between the sections. Add ½in (1cm) for the seam allowance to calculate the size to cut your filler piece.

Filler pieces.

## Avoiding a striped quilt

In traditional piecing you typically assemble a common block, such as a Nine-Patch, by first sewing the pieces into rows, and then sewing the rows together to create the block.

With improv piecing, whether ruler or ruler-free, sewing the pieces into rows and assembling them into the block may feel like the best choice, however, by doing this you will potentially create a block that gives the illusion of stripes, or draws attention to the rows. Using the alternative assembly method below avoids this illusion of making your blocks appear "striped." Use this method or similar practice when joining pieces, units, segments, or blocks in an improv quilt.

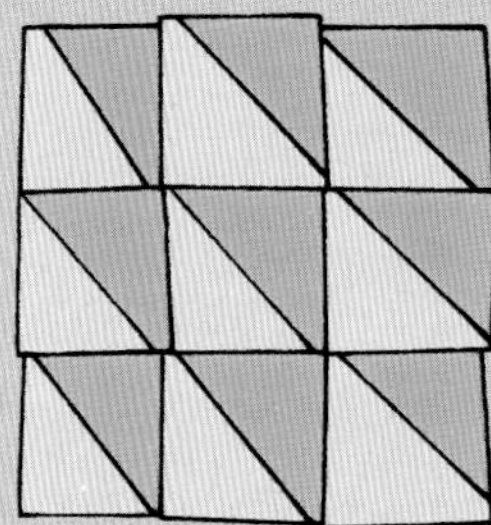

**Step 1** Assemble a Four-Patch, Two-Patch, and a row of three.

**Step 2** Attach the Four-Patch and the Two-patch together.

**Step 3** To complete the Nine-Patch assembly, attach the row of three to the segment created in step 2.

# 1 Color play

I am going to assume you are a fellow color-loving quilter if you are reading this book. I am also going to assume that you are curious about improving the color selection and placement for your quilts.

My recommendation is to not try to learn new color skills at the same time as learning new improv design and technical skills. We will first look at color and how colors interact with each other before we dive into improv technical skills.

We all know the basic primary and secondary colors: red, orange, yellow, green, blue, and violet. I want to encourage you to add tertiary colors—the in-betweens—and work with a 12-color color wheel.

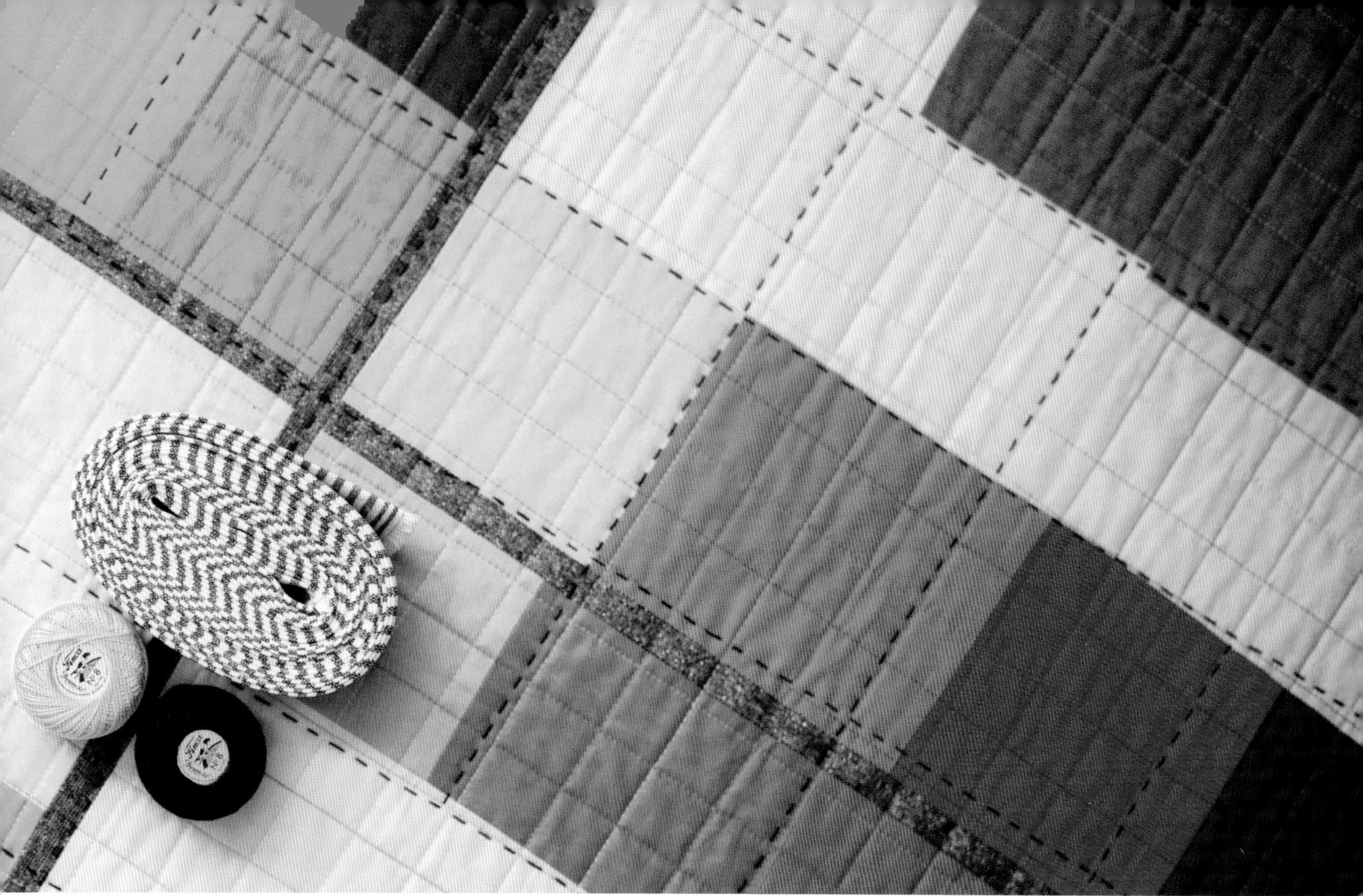

The tertiary colors are red-orange, yellow-orange, yellow-green, blue-green, blue-violet, and red-violet. You may know some of these colors by their street names: red-orange as coral or peach; yellow-orange as apricot or gold; yellow-green as chartreuse or lime green; blue-green as mint, aqua, teal, or turquoise; blue-violet as periwinkle or indigo; and red-violet as plum or magenta. I love tertiary colors and favor them in my own work.

Another important part of color is value. Value is how dark or light a hue is. For example, within the red hue you can have a dark value like burgundy, or a light value like pale pink. It will be important to use value to create movement when applying color to your quilts.

# COLOR HARMONIES

Let's take a look at color harmonies. There are color combinations that scientifically work better together. Color harmonies give us a guide on what colors work well together.

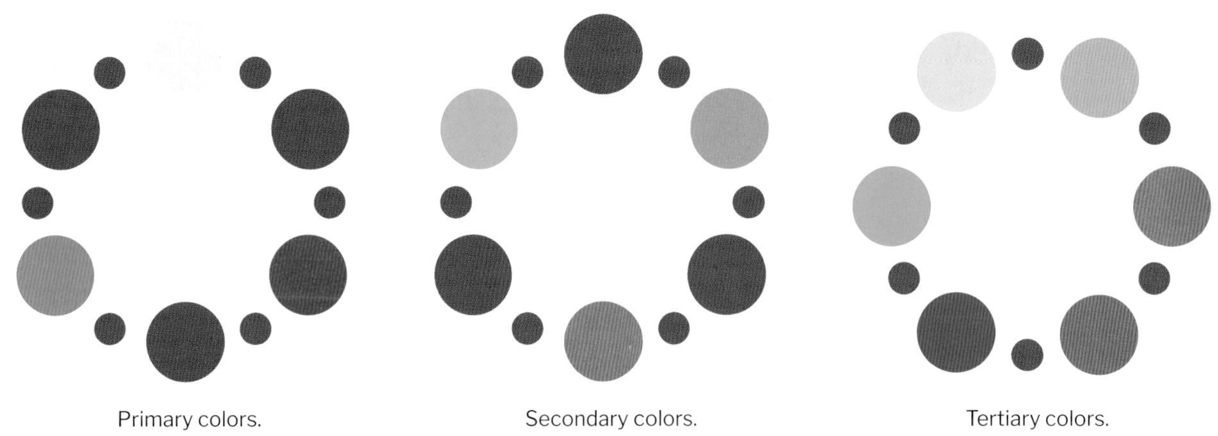

Primary colors. Secondary colors. Tertiary colors.

## Complementary

You are probably familiar with the most basic color harmony: complementary colors. A complementary color harmony is made up of two colors that sit across from each other on the color wheel. Complementary colors even happen within tertiary colors.

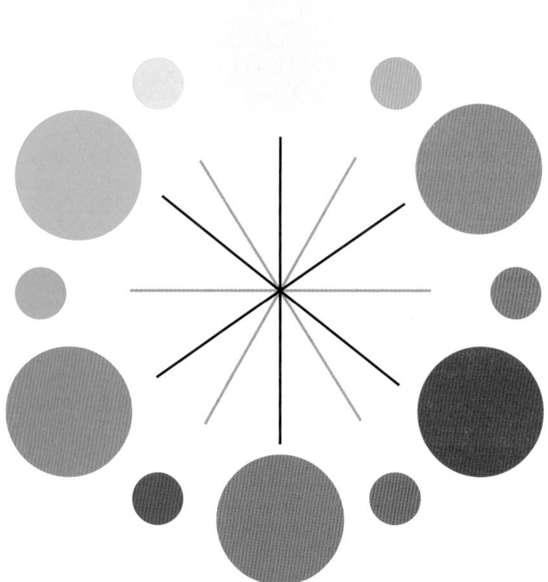

## Split complementary

Now let's make complementary colors a little more interesting and look at split complementary colors. This color harmony allows us to select a primary or secondary color and pair it with two different tertiary colors. Or pair a tertiary color with a primary and a secondary color. We now have three colors in the color harmony. Three is more interesting than two.

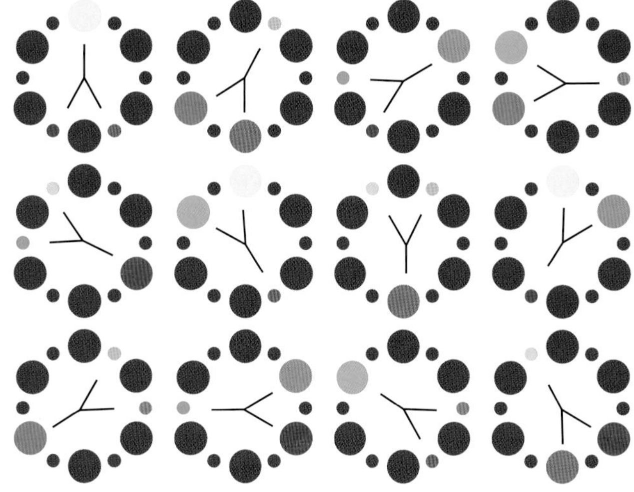

## Analogous

I like to refer to analogous color harmony as the "best friend color harmony." All these colors already sit next to each other and go together. Typically, an analogous color harmony contains three to four colors. Analogous colors are often referred to as warm colors or cool colors. However, these color harmonies can cross over and contain both warm and cool colors.

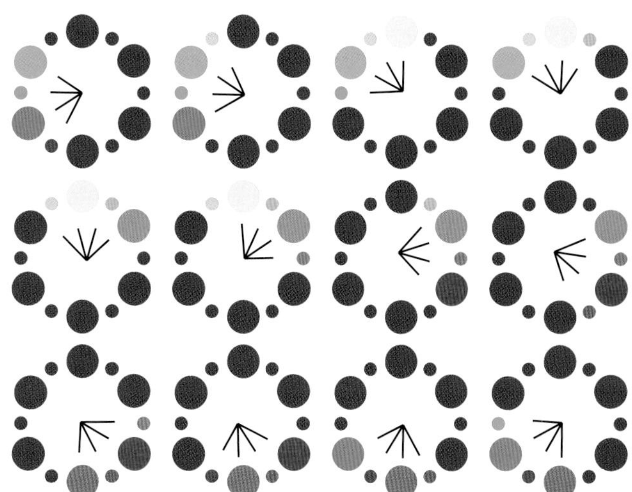

## Split analogous

You guessed it, time to make analogous color harmony more interesting. Let's introduce these color friends to the friend-of-a-friend. Or look at every other color on the color wheel. Maybe they are in the same warm or cool color group, but they don't regularly play together. This makes a more interesting dynamic. Split analogous colors still contain three to four colors in their harmony.

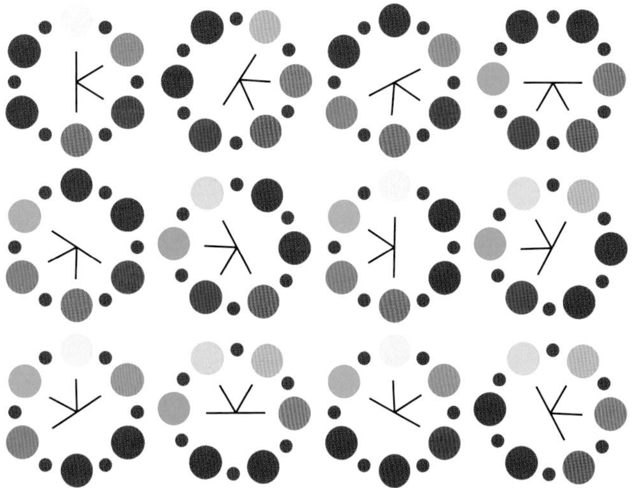

## Triadic

Even if you never knew triadic color harmonies by that name, you are familiar with two triadic color harmonies already—primary and secondary colors are two examples of triadic color harmonies. Let's look at sets of tertiary colors to add more triadic color harmonies to your toolbox.

Triadic color harmony consists of three colors, thus the name "TRI"adic. Create the harmonies by using an equilateral triangle to group the colors.

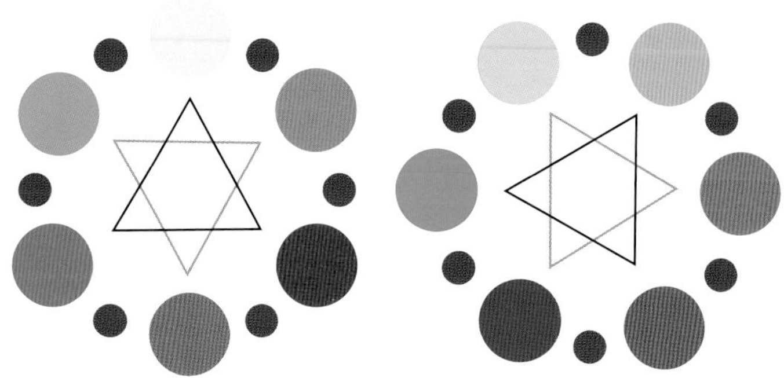

Triadic color combinations.

## Tetradic

The last color harmony we will look at is tetradic. There are two versions of tetradic harmony: one is made with a square (not shown here), and the one we will look at is made with a rectangle.

A tetradic color harmony captures two complementary harmonies and puts them in the same harmony, giving the harmony four colors. Three harmonies can be created with primary plus secondary colors, and three additional harmonies can be created with tertiary colors.

Tetradic color combinations.

I want you to remember these color harmonies when you get into more advanced design and improv work. This chapter will be here for you to reference as needed to help you create beautiful color stories for your quilts.

| COLOR HARMONY | DESCRIPTION | INCLUDED COLORS |
|---|---|---|
| **Primary** | The three colors that can not be made by mixing any other colors. The base of all other colors; all colors can be made by mixing. | Red (R) \| Yellow (Y) \| Blue (B) |
| **Secondary** | Made by mixing adjacent primary colors: R+Y=Orange, Y+B=Green, and B+R=Violet. | Orange (O) \| Green (G) \| Violet (V) |
| **Tertiary** | Created by mixing adjacent primary and secondary colors from the 6-color rainbow: R + O = Red-Orange, Y + O = Yellow-Orange, Y + G = Yellow-Green, B + G = Blue-Green, B + V = Blue-Violet, and V + R = Red-Violet. These are the other six colors of the 12-color color wheel. | Red-Orange (RO) \| Yellow-Orange (YO) \| Yellow-Green (YG) \| Blue-Green (BG) \| Blue-Violet (BV) \| Red-Violet (RV) |
| **Complementary** | Colors that sit across the color wheel from each other. Primary + secondary or two tertiary colors. | Y+V \| YO+BV \| O+B \| RO+BG \| R+G \| RV+YG |
| **Split complementary** | A color plus the adjacent colors on either side of its complement. | Y+BV+RV \| YO+B+V \| O+BG+BV \| RO+G+B<br>R+YG+BG \| RV+Y+G \| V+YO+YG \| BV+O+Y<br>B+RO+YO \| BG+R+O \| G+RO+RV \| YG+R+V |
| **Analogous** | A group of 3–4 adjacent colors on the color wheel. Typically made up of primary + secondary + 1–2 tertiary colors. | G+BG+B+BV \| YG+G+BG+B \| Y+YG+G+BG<br>YO+Y+YG+G \| O+YO+Y+YG \| RO+O+YO+Y<br>R+RO+O+YO \| RV+R+RO+O \| V+RV+R+RO<br>BV+V+RV+R \| B+BV+V+RV \| BG+B+BV+V |

*Table continues on the next page.*

| COLOR HARMONY | DESCRIPTION | INCLUDED COLORS |
|---|---|---|
| Split analogous | A group of 3–4 colors adjacent in either the 6-color rainbow or the 6 tertiary colors. They appear as split, or every other color, in the 12-color color wheel. | Y+O+R+V \| YO+RO+RV+BV \| O+R+V+B<br>RO+RV+BV+BG \| R+V+B+G \| RV+BV+BG+YG<br>V+B+G+Y \| BV+BG+YG+YO \| B+G+Y+O<br>BG+YG+YO+RO \| G+Y+O+R \| YG+YO+RO+RV |
| Triadic | Consists of 3 tertiary colors connected by an equilateral triangle. | R+Y+B \| O+G+V<br>YO+RV+BG \| YG+RO+BV |
| Tetradic | Groups of 4 colors, either from the 6-color rainbow or the tertiary colors, connected by a rectangle. | Y+O+V+B \| O+R+B+G \| R+V+G+Y<br>YG+YO+RV+BV \| YO+RO+BV+BG<br>RO+RV+BG+YG |

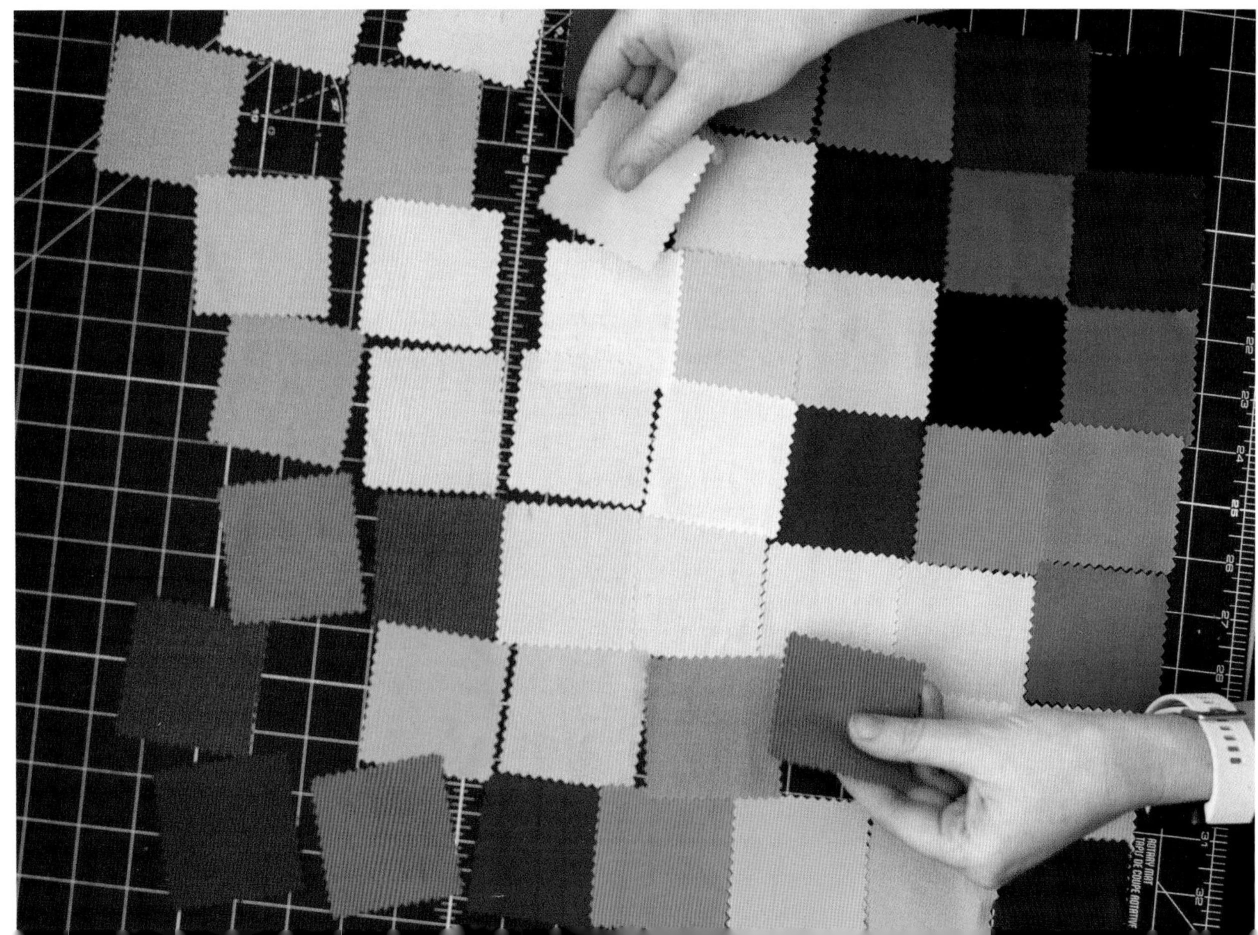

# Applying color to your quilt

**Planning**

When applying color to your quilt there are several approaches you can take. You can use a coloring sheet, see for example pages 124–127. This works well when sewing a traditional or block-based quilt as the outcome is predictable and a coloring sheet is easy to produce. Coloring sheets are provided for projects 1, 3, 5, and 7.

However, if you are working with a more improv approach to the design, it might be difficult to make a coloring sheet of an unknown outcome. In this instance, using a broad location of where a color may land is a better approach. If you are comfortable with paper and colored pencils you can still make a coloring sheet—the piecing will just not be specified. It may also be helpful to identify color locations on your design wall. You can do this by using tape or string to designate sections or by placing bits of fabric to mark where colors will land in the design.

Revisit your color plan throughout the making of your quilt. To do this, compare your coloring sheet to your design wall. You can also snap a photograph on your phone of your quilt in progress and use an app to mark different color sections as you build your quilt.

**Color harmonies**

If you are working with a block-based design, you can easily include multiple color harmonies in a single quilt. Work each block as a separate color story and the fabrics adjacent to each other in a block will play nicely together. You will end up with a colorful and scrappy quilt because each block will have a different color story. This technique is shown well in project 8 (page 92). Alternatively, you can apply the same color harmony to an entire quilt for a less scrappy look, like in project 7 (page 86).

**Color blocking**

Instead of applying the colors in a mixed-up, scrappy fashion, try applying the colors with a color-block approach. Group like colors together and move in sections across the quilt. Create sections with definite boundaries and complementary colors adjacent to each other for a high-contrast appearance. Color blocking is shown in the sample quilts for both projects 4 and 6 (pages 56 and 76).

**Color gradient**

To achieve a softer, painterly appearance, place color groups next to each other in rainbow order within their harmony, and use overlap and soft edges for color bleed into the next section. Project 1 (page 28) uses a color gradient layout with an analogous color harmony.

**Color value**

Use color value—light and dark versions of your selected colors—to create movement and depth. Moving through value creates an ombre effect and adds dimension to your quilt. Using high-contrast values next to each other adds interest in the design. Projects 2 and 3 (pages 34 and 48) use value placement to organize flow in the composition.

**Areas of interest**

There are other ways to add interest to your quilt. Even after you have most of your fabric or blocks on your design wall/surface, you can still add areas of interest. The viewer's eye will be drawn to high-contrast areas. Choose complementary colors or value differences for contrast.

Add out-of-place colors or values. If you have made an entire quilt with pastels, consider adding a dark value in small amounts in just a few places. Or, in an area of only warm colors, add in a cool color. The added pieces do not need to be large—just enough to make the viewer take a second look. Areas of interest keep the eye moving in project 10's quilt (page 110). Color blocking near complementary colors, high value contrast, and out-of-place colors all keep the composition interesting. In project 5 (page 68), cool colors are used as small filler pieces contrasting with the overall warm color harmony of the quilt.

# Project 1: Irish Chain

Let's apply color harmony to a simple block-based quilt. The Irish Chain is a classic quilt with a clean, modern look.

You will work with a more complex color harmony to complete the color story. Focus on arranging your selected colors into a gradient with both color order and value in mind. You will be making improv color placement decisions, but measuring, cutting, and piecing traditionally.

Remember, your selected color harmony may be different than mine as your fabric stash is different than mine. Your project will illustrate your preferred colors and your unique fabric stash.

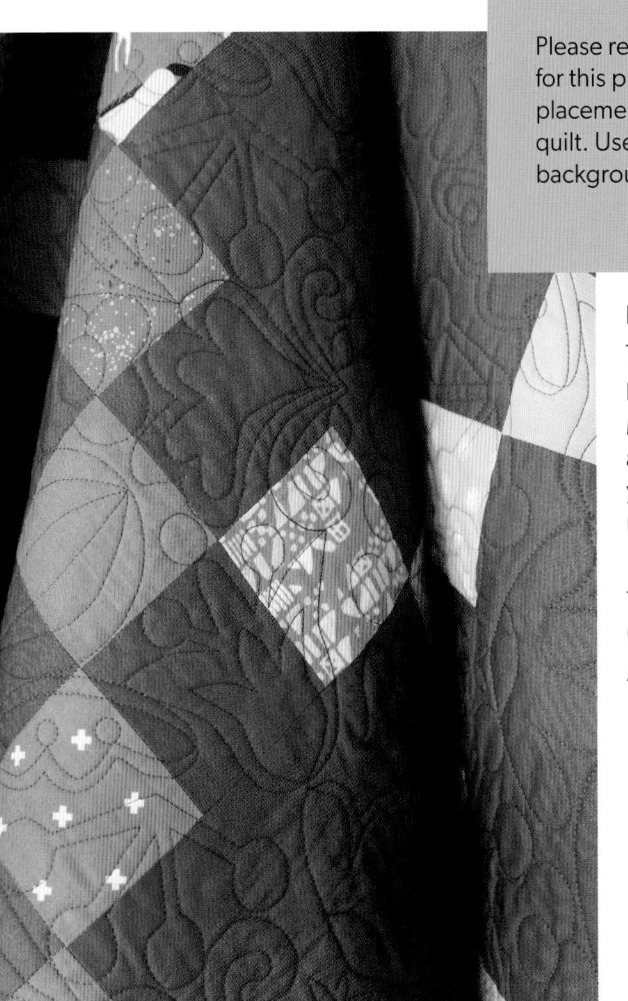

Please read through all the instructions for this project before starting. Color placement is the improv decision for this quilt. Use 75–125 unique fabrics plus a background fabric.

## REQUIREMENTS

The sample quilt uses 125 unique fabrics plus 2¾yd (2.5m) of background fabric.

My selected color harmony is split analogous (see page 23), including yellow-green, yellow-orange, red-orange, and red-violet.

The finished quilt is 62 x 62in (157.5 x 157.5cm).

Aim for a finished quilt size of a similar size.

## Color decisions

Select a complex color harmony—split complementary, split analogous, triadic, or tetradic—to build your color palette. Select a background fabric that works well with your selected color harmony. Neutrals work with almost any harmony, but you could also select the complement if using a split analogous harmony.

Take a copy of the Irish Chain coloring sheet on page 124. Divide the coloring sheet into three or four sections based on your selected color harmony. The sections do not need to be even or equal. Apply the colors from your palette to the coloring sheet using colored pencils.

Begin with a single color in each section and move toward the next color in the harmony by overlapping color sections where they meet.

## Cutting

**From color fabrics:**

- Using your coloring sheet to identify color placement, begin cutting squares for your Nine-Patch blocks.
- Cut 125 color fabric squares, each measuring 3½ x 3½in (9 x 9cm).

As you cut squares, place them on your design wall/surface in the section designated for that color.

**From background fabric:**

- Cut 9 width-of-fabric (WOF) strips, each measuring 3½in (9cm), then sub-cut:
  - 100 squares, each measuring 3½ x 3½in (9 x 9cm).
- Cut 6 WOF strips, each measuring 9½in (24cm), and then sub-cut:
  - 24 squares, each measuring 9½ x 9½in (24 x 24cm).

## Assemble—blocks

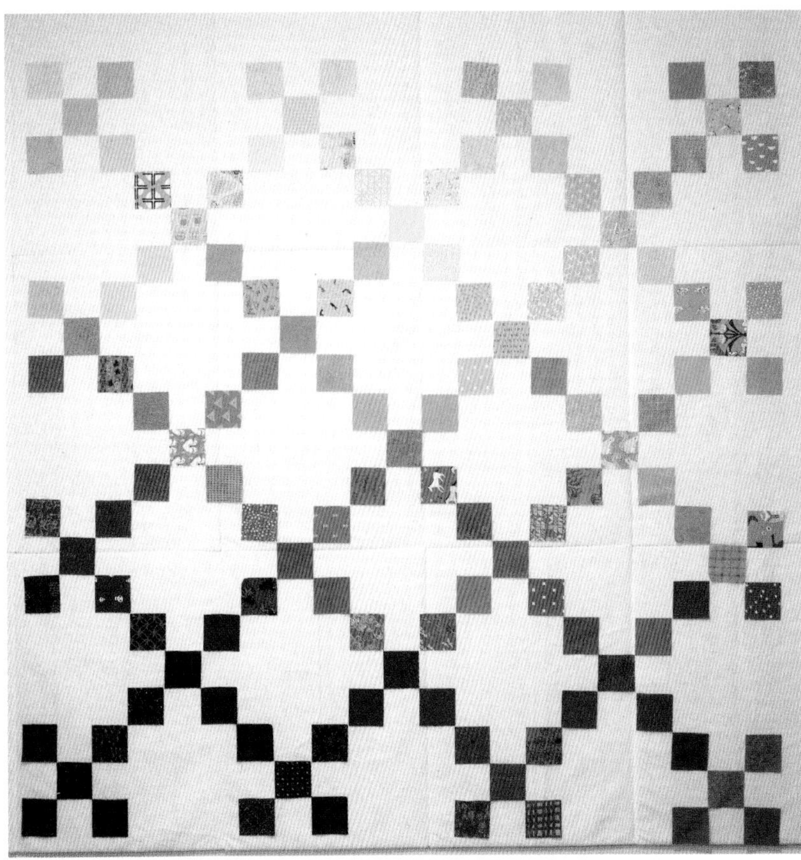

**Step 1** Arrange the Nine-Patch block components on your design wall/surface.

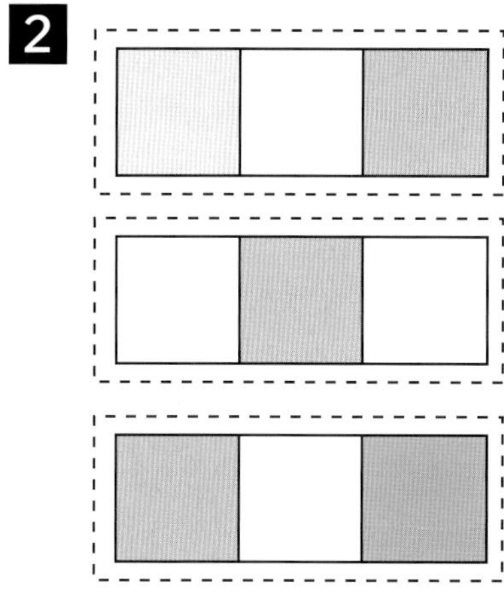

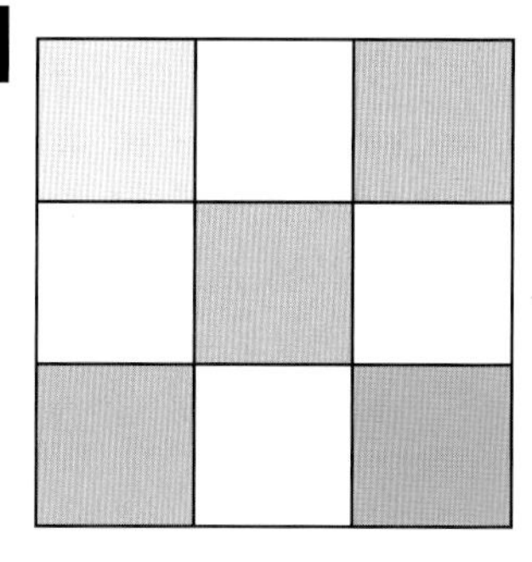

**Step 2** Using a traditional Nine-Patch method, assemble rows for each block. Sew the right sides together and press all seams open.

**Step 3** Assemble the rows together (as shown on the left). Sew the rows right sides together and press all seams open.

**Step 4** Trim the blocks to 9½ x 9½in (24 x 24cm), unfinished.

## Assemble—quilt top

**Step 5** Arrange the blocks within your color sections according to your Irish Chain coloring sheet.

**Step 6** Join the blocks into rows. Sew right sides together and press all seams open.

**Step 7** Assemble the rows together. Sew the right sides together and press all seams open.

## Finishing the quilt

See notes on quilt finishing, pages 116–122.

The sample quilt is finished with a longarm quilted pantograph and machine binding.

*Quilted by Cara Cansler, Sew Colorado Quilting, Westminster, CO.*

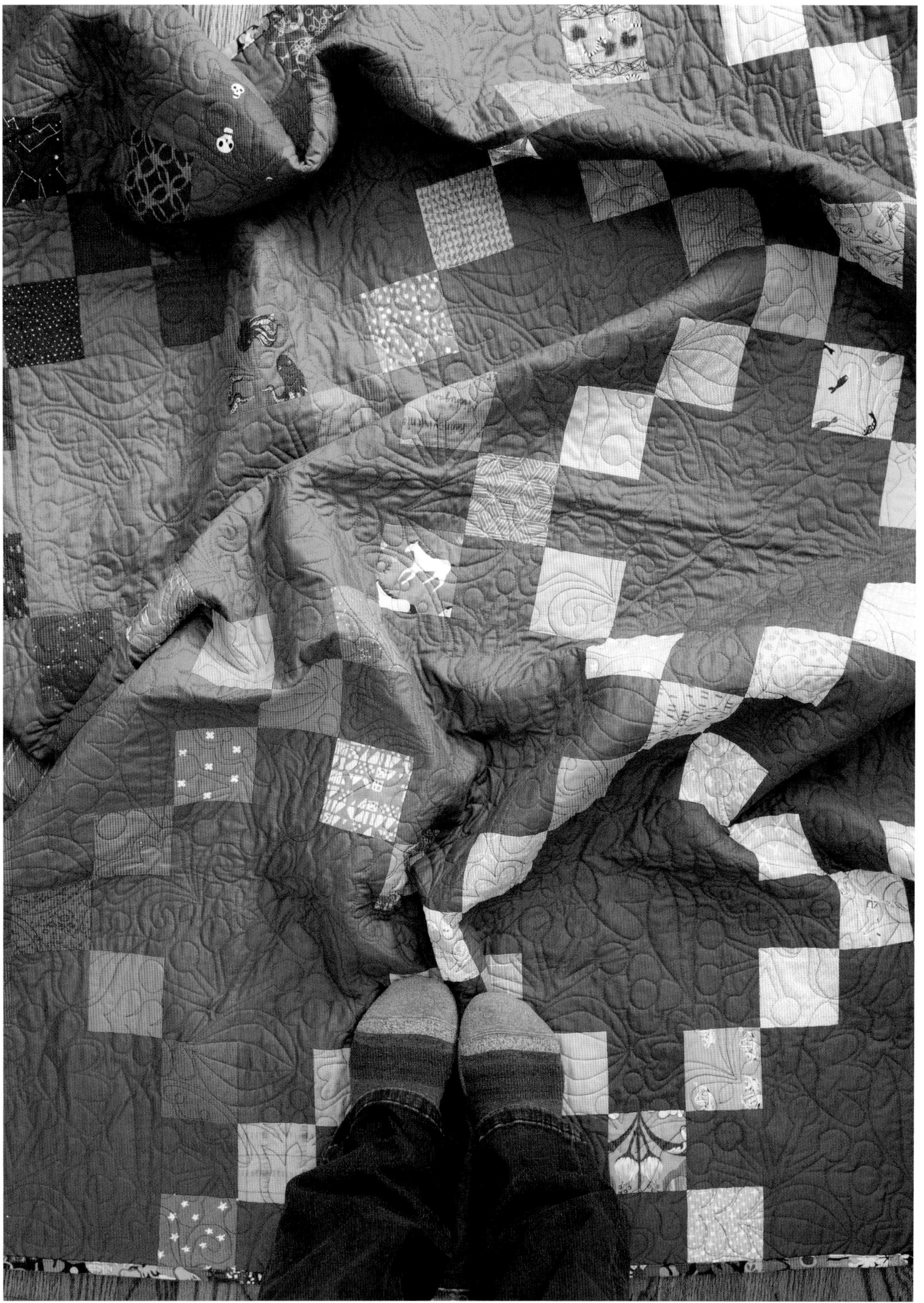

# Project 2: Your Rainbow in Squares

Using your colorful fabric stash you will create a quilt that represents your rainbow, or your preferred colors. Your fabric stash looks different than mine so your finished project will look different. Use whatever fabric you have—if it's already in your stash, you probably like it. Solid, woven, or print fabric will all work for this project. My project is made with my collection of solid, linen, and shot cotton fabrics. If you do not have a large enough stash you can always request pieces of fabric from friends or purchase a charm pack of 5in (12.5cm) squares from a fabric manufacturer.

If you love jewel tones, your rainbow will be saturated, deep colors. If you prefer muted colors, you will have a dusty rainbow. If there's a color that you really don't like using, or you don't have any in your stash, you can skip that color in your rainbow.

Let's get started!

Please read through all the instructions for this project before starting. The improv decision for this quilt is the color placement. Select 75–175 unique color fabrics, plus up to 2yd (1.8m) of border fabric.

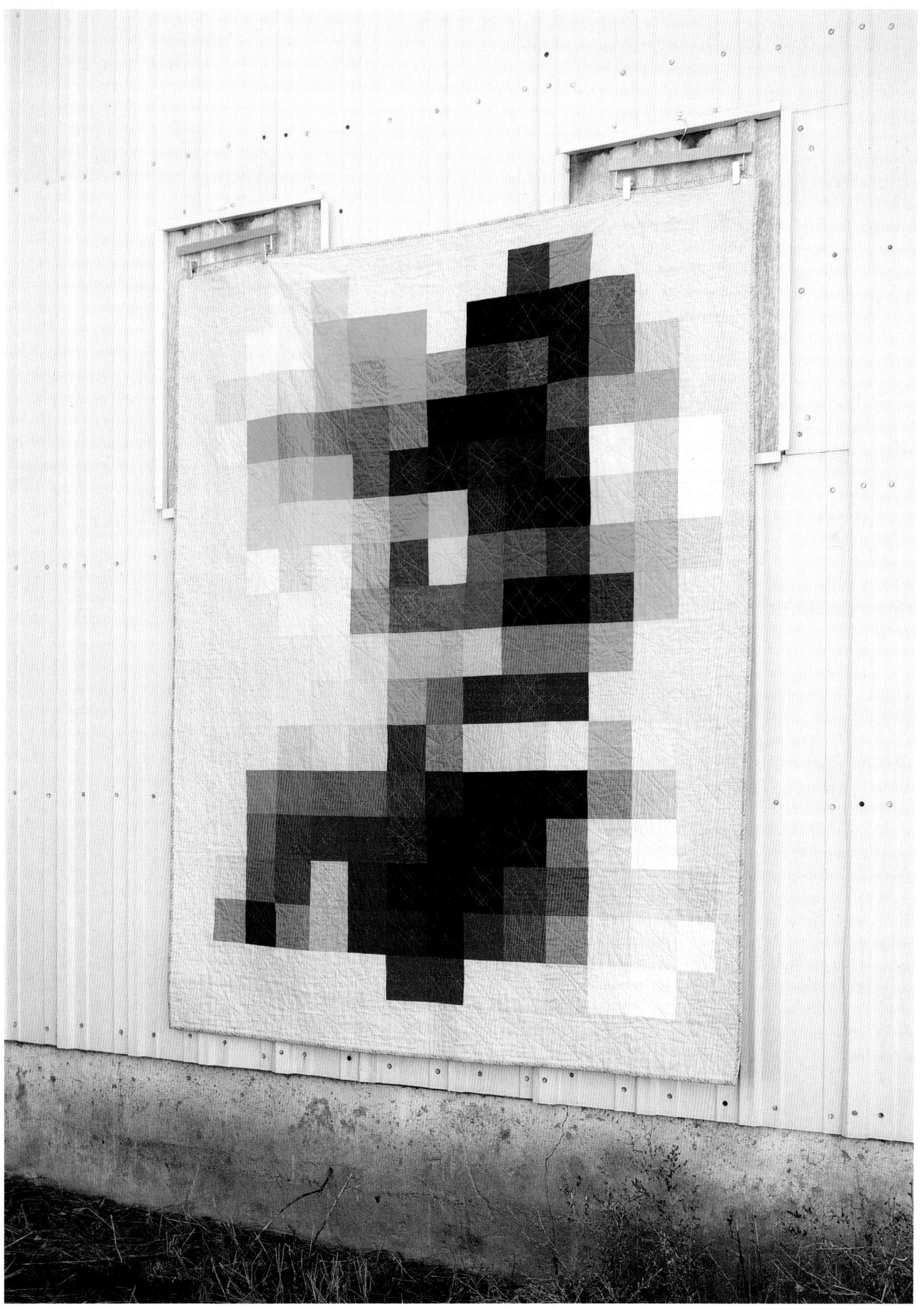

**REQUIREMENTS**

The sample uses 149 unique fabrics, plus border fabric. Because I favor tertiary colors, I have sub-divided some of my tertiary colors into additional categories to create a total of 18 color categories.

The finished sample quilt size is 67 x 80in (170 x 203cm).

Aim for your finished quilt to be around 50 x 60in (127 x 152cm) to 75 x 90in (190 x 229cm).

## Cutting

Cut a single 5 x 5in (12.5 x 12.5cm) square from each color fabric.

## Color sorting

Sort your squares into color categories. Suggested categories are:

- Red
- Red-orange
- Orange
- Yellow-orange
- Yellow
- Yellow-green
- Green
- Blue-green
- Blue
- Blue-violet
- Violet
- Red-violet
- Cool neutrals (gray)
- Black
- White
- Warm neutrals (beige)

My categories are: white, beige, violet-red (plum), red-violet (magenta), red, red-orange (coral), orange-red (peach), orange, yellow-orange, yellow, yellow-green, green, green-blue (turquoise), blue-green (teal), blue, blue-violet, gray, and black.

You may also see that I have left out violet completely. This is because my stash contains only blue-violet or red-violet fabrics.

## Value sorting

Next, arrange your color categories by value. Value is how light or dark a color is. Arrange each color category from lightest to darkest value, as shown in the photograph below.

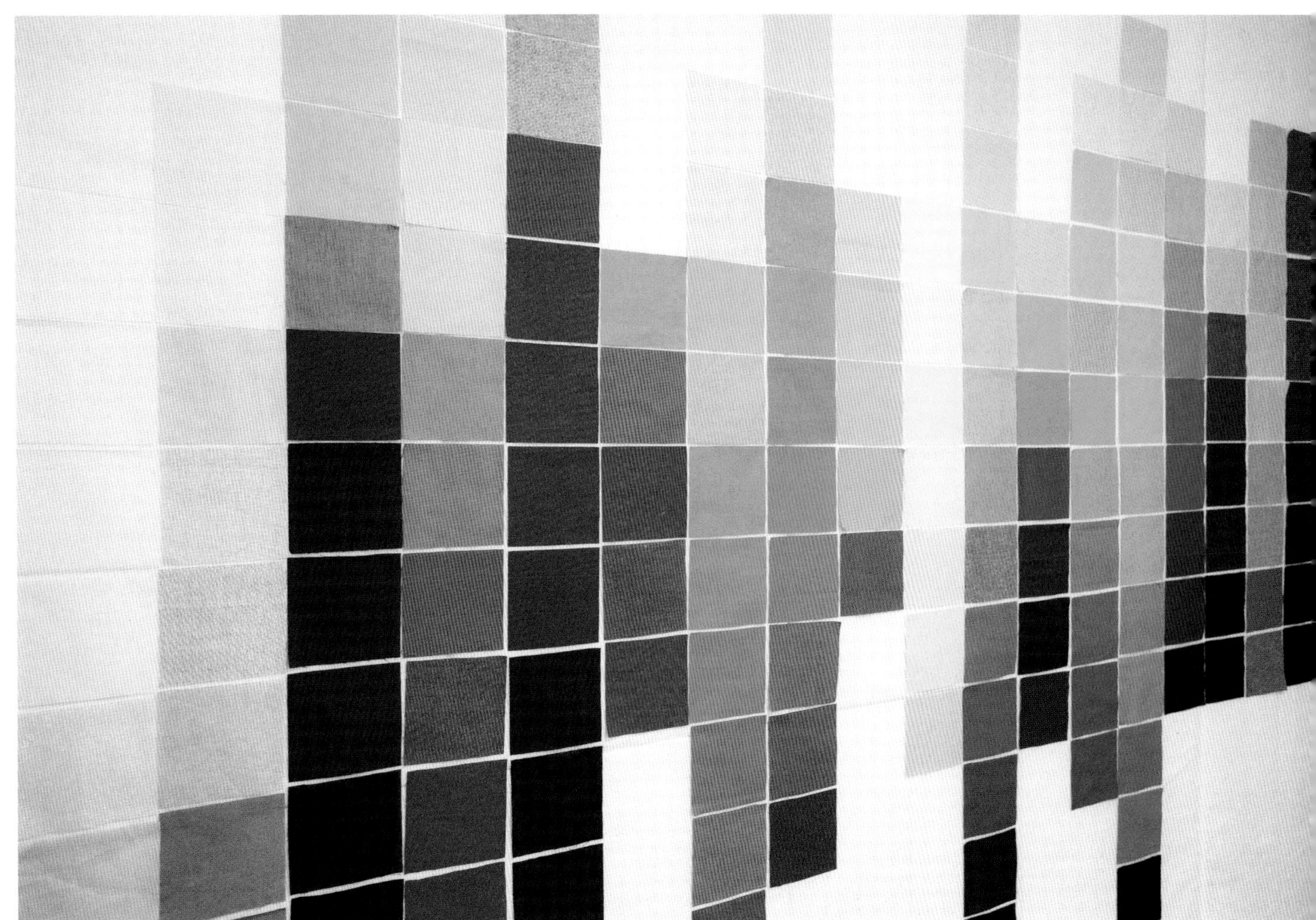

## Design-wall play

Play with multiple shapes within each section and arrangements of your fabric squares to create a rainbow gradient you love. This is *your* rainbow, and if you find there is a color or square that doesn't play nicely, you can still remove it from your design wall. However, in this situation it may be best to add more color as opposed to removing a color. Try it both ways.

**Step 1** Divide your design wall into sections using tape or string. For the sample quilt the design wall is divided into quadrants. You may choose to divide into more than four sections; six or twelve may work better for you. Divide your sections as a grid or a pie. Place your colors in a rainbow gradient. Aim to place colors into a color-blocking arrangement instead of grouping like colors in rows or columns of each hue. The sample quilt begins with warm colors in the lower quadrants; red-orange and yellow on the left, and violet-red and magenta on the right.

**Step 2** Place darker values of each color block and work outward with lighter values. Incorporate neutral colors into your rainbow or separate them into their own areas. When the bottom quadrants were filled with warm color squares, I began the upper quadrants using the darkest green values. The yellow from the lower left phases into yellow-green in the upper left.

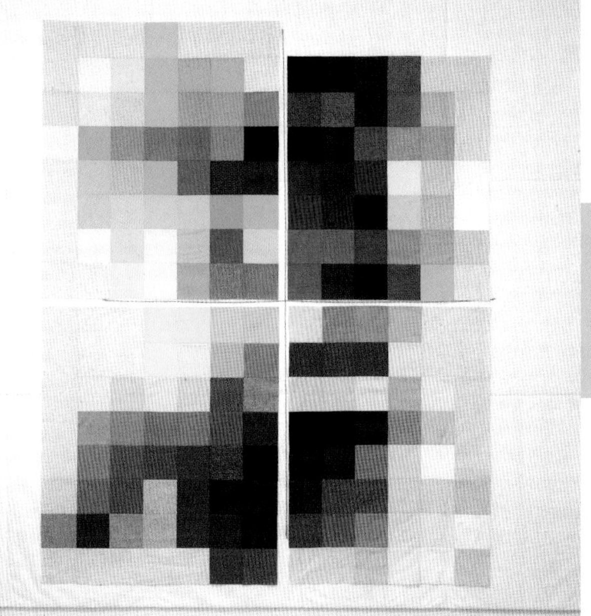

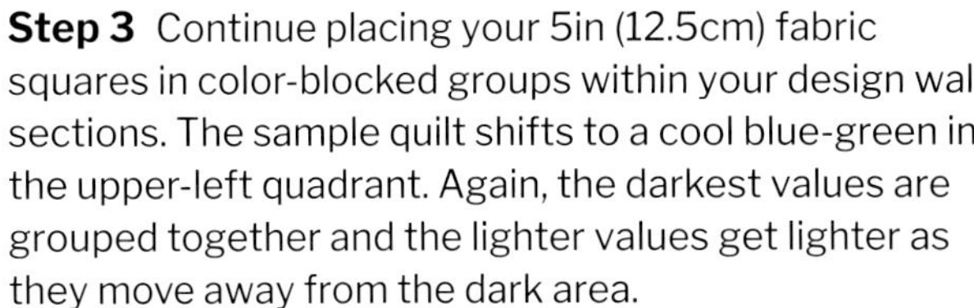

**Step 3** Continue placing your 5in (12.5cm) fabric squares in color-blocked groups within your design wall sections. The sample quilt shifts to a cool blue-green in the upper-left quadrant. Again, the darkest values are grouped together and the lighter values get lighter as they move away from the dark area.

**Step 4** Complete the placement of the 5in (12.5cm) fabric squares. The sample quilt finishes the upper right quadrant with the darkest blue values and more cool neutrals.

**Step 5** Begin assembling the design wall sections into groups that create large squares or rectangles. The sample quilt uses rows and columns to easily construct each quadrant. However, the design is not symmetrical and it appears to have jagged edges because of the placement of the color squares versus the surrounding background fabric.

**Step 6** Add the borders around the rainbow squares after filling in any jagged edges. For narrow borders choose a 5in (12.5cm) width. A 10in (25.5cm) border will frame your rainbow squares and increase the size of your finished quilt. Borders do not need to be symmetrical. Attach all borders right sides together. Press open.

## Finishing the quilt

See notes on quilt finishing, pages 116–122.

The sample quilt is quilted on a domestic machine with an edge-to-edge, walking-foot design. It is hand bound.

# 2

# Improv piecing: Ruler-cut

"You will always be successful if you sew a straight edge to another straight edge."

Now that you are comfortable with color harmonies, you have defined your rainbow colors, and have practiced color placement, you can learn the next step to putting together a unique improv quilt. There are a few skills to add to your toolbox when it comes to improv piecing. The first skill we will look at is ruler-cut piecing. "Ruler-cut" and "straight edge" will be used interchangeably.

You will be using a ruler to make all the cuts for this style of improv piecing. There is just one rule you need to know for this skill: you will always be successful if you sew a straight edge to another straight edge. It's as simple as that.

Before you sew any pieces together, always trim the edges that you are joining using your ruler. This ensures that your quilt top will lay flat when it is pressed after sewing your seams.

Let's look at some common scenarios where you may use ruler-cut improv piecing.

# BASICS OF RULER-CUT IMPROV PIECING

## Log Cabin

A traditional Log Cabin block is a great example of where ruler-cut improv piecing can be applied. You may also hear the improv version of this block referred to as a "wonky Log Cabin." All the edges are still cut with your ruler, but there is no regard to the corner angles. You do not need to create 90-degree corners unless you are intentionally placing one somewhere in your improv work. Remember that sewing a straight edge to another straight edge will guarantee success. The wonky Log Cabin is built the same way a traditional Log Cabin block is constructed.

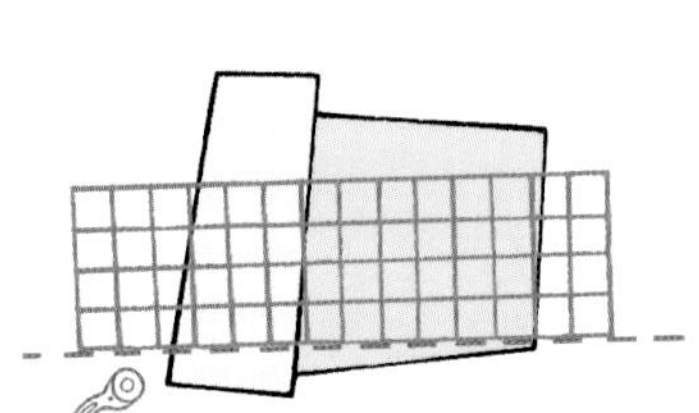

**Step 1** Beginning with the center, add a piece to one side. Press open. Trim the edge that will receive the next piece.

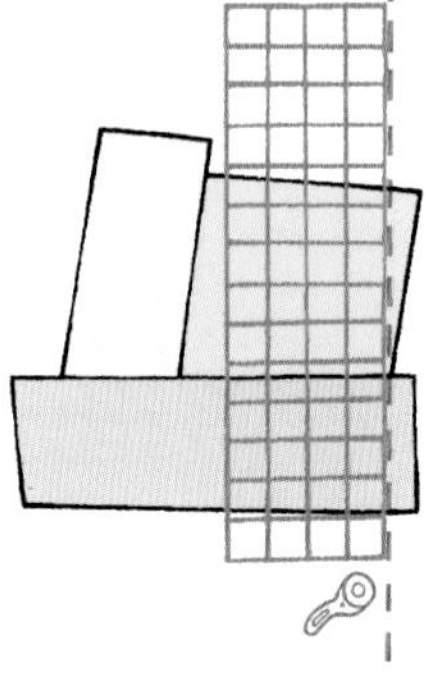

**Step 2** Working around the center, add the next piece. Press open. Trim the edge that will receive the next piece.

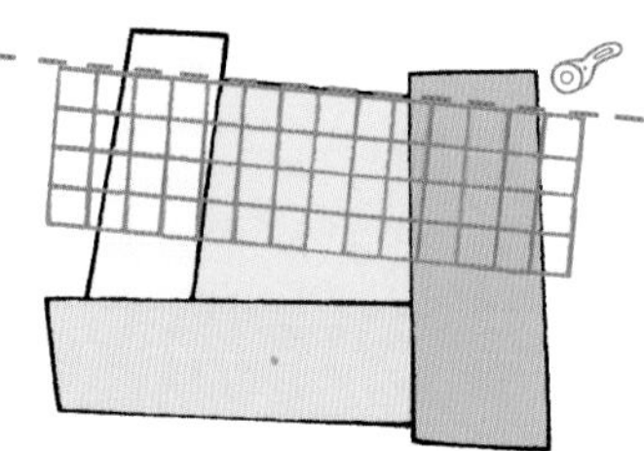

**Step 3** Add another piece to the next side. Press open. Trim the next edge as before.

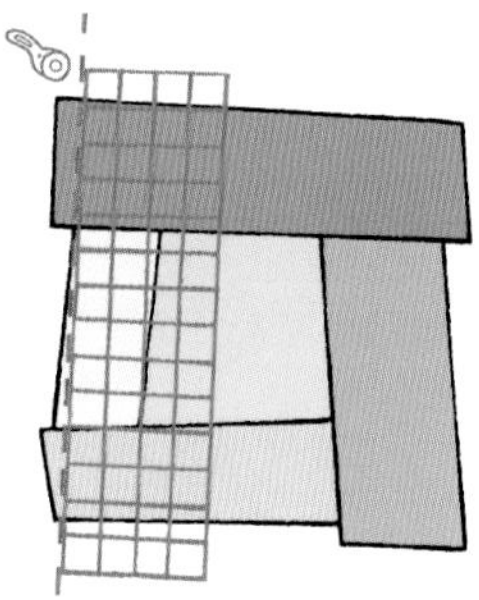

**Step 4** Continue adding pieces, working around the block. Press open.

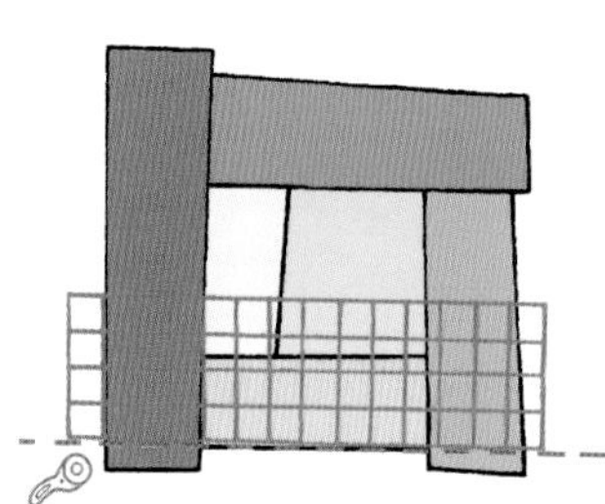

**Step 5** Remember that for a flat block, you must trim every edge receiving a piece before you sew.

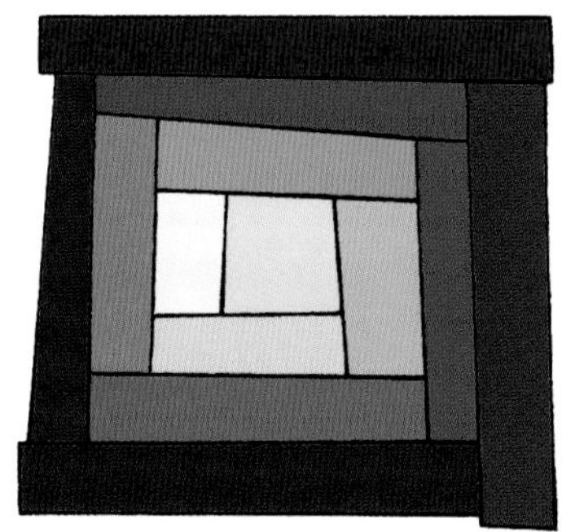

**Step 6** Continue trimming edges and adding pieces until your Log Cabin has grown to the desired size.

A variation on the Log Cabin block is the Courthouse Steps block. This, too, can be made using the ruler-cut improv skill. The same trimming method can be used to add any improv pieces that would otherwise be straight.

## Triangles and diagonal cuts

Making Half Square Triangles (HSTs) or other traditional quilting triangle shapes—such as Flying Geese, equilateral triangles, diamonds and Half Rectangle Triangles (HRTs)—can also be made with the ruler-cut improv technique.

Always use your ruler to trim both edges that will be joined together before sewing a seam. The angle at which you place your ruler for cutting can determine how wonky or off-set your diagonal seam will be.

Make your diagonal cut with your ruler first and then approximate the diagonal cut on your second piece of fabric to end up with a shape you are aiming for.

### *HSTs or HRTs*

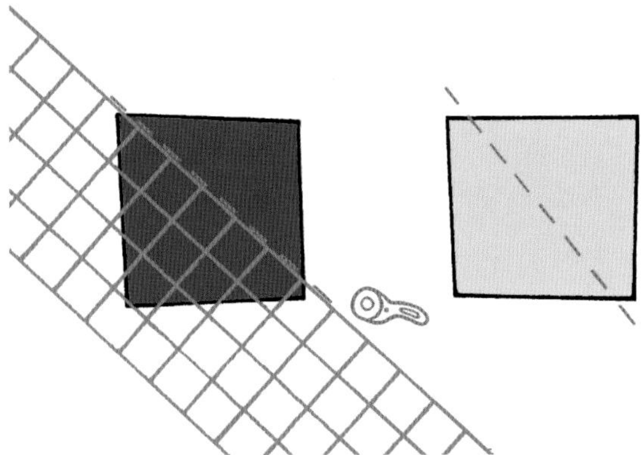

**Step 1** Using your ruler, diagonally cut two contrasting squares or rectangles.

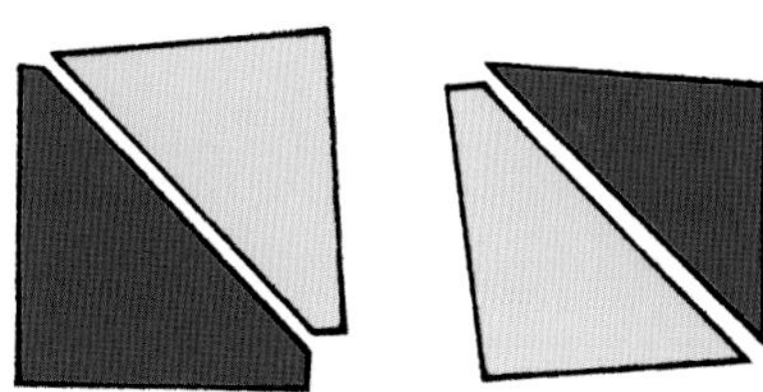

**Step 2** Pair each diagonally cut section of fabric 1 with a diagonally cut section of fabric 2.

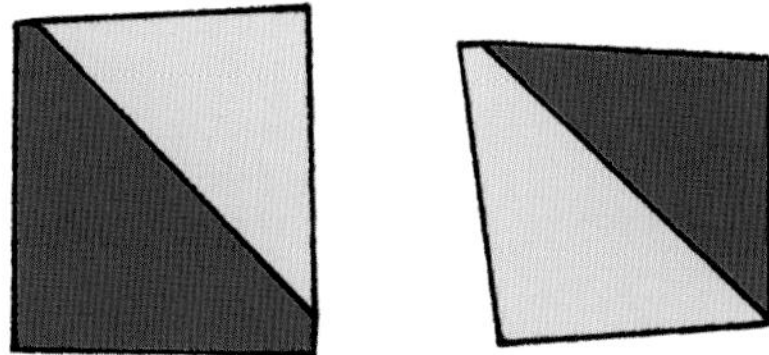

**Step 3** Sew the pairs right sides together along the diagonal using a ¼in (5mm) seam allowance. Press open.

## Stripes

When piecing stripes with the ruler-cut improv technique, you will be working with wedges because your corners are not 90 degrees. When laying out your wedge shapes, be aware that it is easy to create an arc if you place all the wide ends on the same side and all the small ends on the other side. Alternate which side the wide end sits on to create a field of stripes as opposed to a striped arc. Of course, there may be times when you want to create an arc (see page 85).

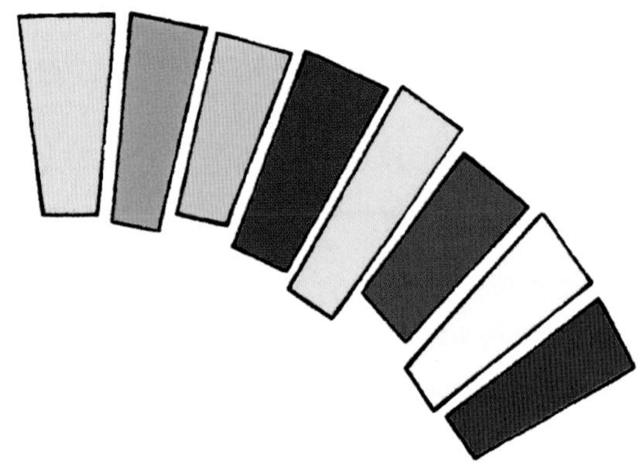

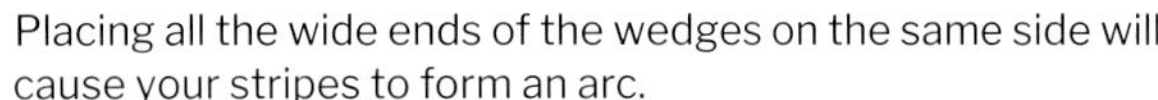

Placing all the wide ends of the wedges on the same side will cause your stripes to form an arc.

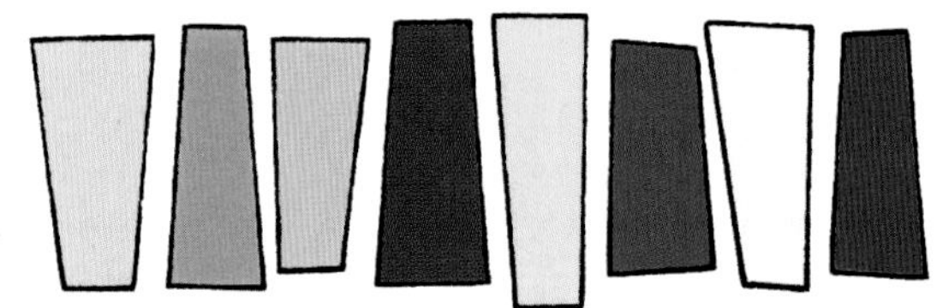

Alternating the wide and narrow ends of your wedges will create a striped panel.

## Piecing ruler-cut improv segments together

Another common instance when ruler-cut improv is useful is when you are putting multiple ruler-cut improv segments or blocks together to create a quilt top. The edges of each segment may not be straight and may have ended up jagged because of the combination of cuts used to assemble the section and the size of fabric pieces used. You can use your ruler-cut improv skill to join the block units together. Trim both edges that will be joined with your straight edge before sewing them together.

When joining segments or blocks together you may need to incorporate filler pieces, see "Tips and tricks: improve your improv" on page 18–19 for more on filler.

Omnigrip

# Project 3: Sawtooth Star

Like the Irish Chain (page 28) where you applied a color harmony to a traditional block and layout, you will now be using the same strategy to apply a color harmony or your own rainbow, but you'll be cutting and piecing using ruler-cut improv.

For this project I use a traditional Sawtooth Star block. This block consists of squares and Half Square Triangles (HSTs).

Please read through all the instructions for this project before starting. This quilt uses a traditional block and layout to enable you to practice your straight-edge improv cutting and piecing skills and apply a color harmony or your rainbow. The goal of this project is to strengthen color play and apply ruler-cut improv piecing to a traditional block.

**REQUIREMENTS**

The sample uses over 50 unique fabrics, plus approximately 2yd (1.8m) of background fabric.

My selected color harmony is split complementary (see page 22), including the colors blue, green, and red-orange.

The finished sample quilt is 54.5 x 68in (138 x 173cm). Aim for a finished quilt of a similar size.

## Color sketch

First, determine your color harmony. Use any of the color harmonies discussed in chapter 1, or use your own rainbow colors. Using colored pencils to represent your fabric colors, illustrate a coloring sheet of the Sawtooth Star quilt (on page 125) to determine each color location.

Apply colors by moving through both value and color gradients. Create interest by grouping like values together in nearby blocks. This will create a darker area and a lighter area of the quilt. Balance the darker area by adding a small amount of a darker value across the quilt. Center squares and HST units of the Sawtooth Star block creating the star will be part of the color story. Corner squares, HSTs, and sashing will be background fabric.

## Cutting

**From color fabrics:**

Using your coloring sheet to identify color placement, cut color fabrics for your star blocks. In total:

- Cut 20 color fabric center squares using your ruler approximately 6½ x 6½in (16.5 x 16.5cm). Intentionally cut squares without 90-degree corners. Place on design wall according to coloring sheet.
- Cut 80 color fabric squares to use for HSTs. Using your ruler, cut approximately 4 x 4in (10 x 10cm). Intentionally cut squares without 90-degree corners.

**From background fabric:**

- Cut 80 squares for outer corners using your ruler, cut approximately 3½ x 3½in (9 x 9cm). Intentionally cut squares without 90-degree corners.
- Cut 80 squares to use for HSTs. Using your ruler, cut approximately 4 x 4in (10 x 10cm). Intentionally cut squares without 90-degree corners.

Reserve remaining background fabric for sashing.

## Assemble—HSTs

You can refer back to page 45 for more on making ruler-cut HSTs.

**Step 1** Using your ruler, diagonally cut all 160 approximately 4in (10cm) squares; color and background fabrics.

**Step 2** Pair each diagonally cut section of the color fabric with a diagonally cut section of background fabric.

**Step 3** Sew the pairs right sides together along the diagonal using a ¼in (5mm) seam allowance. Press open.

**Step 4** Place the untrimmed HSTs onto your design wall/surface in designated color sections based on your Sawtooth Star coloring sheet.

**Step 5** Add the corner squares to the design wall layout, as pictured below.

# Assemble—blocks

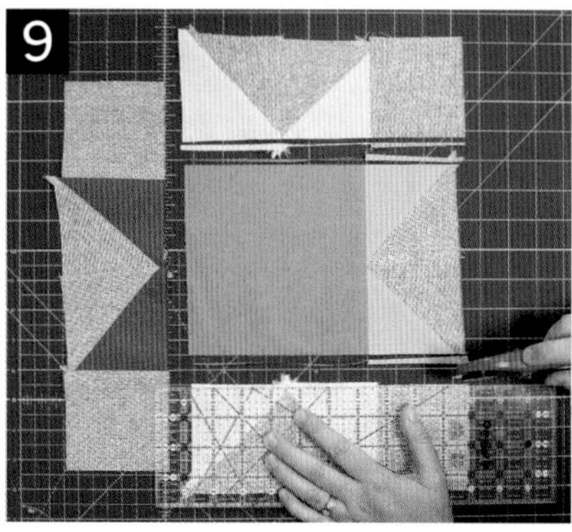

The finished block.

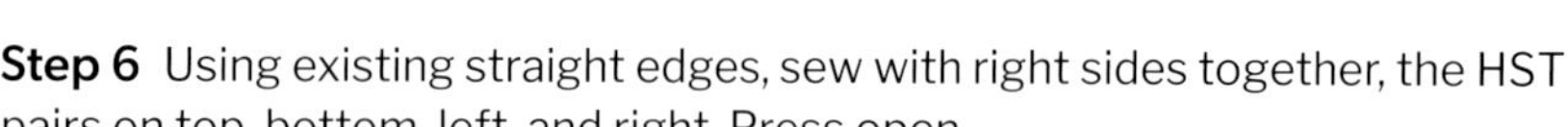

**Step 6** Using existing straight edges, sew with right sides together, the HST pairs on top, bottom, left, and right. Press open.

**Step 7** Using existing straight edges, sew with right sides together, the top and bottom HST pairs + right corner squares, and the left HST pair + left corner squares. Press open.

**Step 8** Using a ruler, trim the inside edge of the right HST pair. Sew right sides together, the right HST pair + center square. Press open.

**Step 9** Using a ruler, trim the inside of the top and bottom HST pair + corner square and trim the top and bottom of the right HST pair + center square. Sew with right sides together, the top and bottom HST pair + corner square to the right HST pair + center square. Press open.

**Step 10** Using a ruler, trim the inside edges of the remaining segments of the block. Sew with right sides together, the left column to the block segment assembled in the previous steps. Press open. Repeat to make 20 blocks.

## Block sashing

**Step 11** From the background fabric, ruler-cut a strip approximately 2in (5cm) wide.

**Step 12** Approximate the height of your Sawtooth Star block. Cut a length of the approximately 2in (5cm) strip to this height.

**Step 13** Using a ruler, trim the right side of your Sawtooth Star block as shown in the illustration. Repeat for all the blocks.

**Step 14** Sew the right sides together of your Sawtooth Star block + right side sashing. Press open.

**Step 15** Approximate the width of your Sawtooth Star block plus right side sashing. Cut a length of the approximately 2in (5cm) strip to this width.

**Step 16** Using a ruler, trim the bottom of your Sawtooth Star block + right sashing.

**Step 17** Sew with right sides together, the Sawtooth Star block and bottom sashing. Press open.

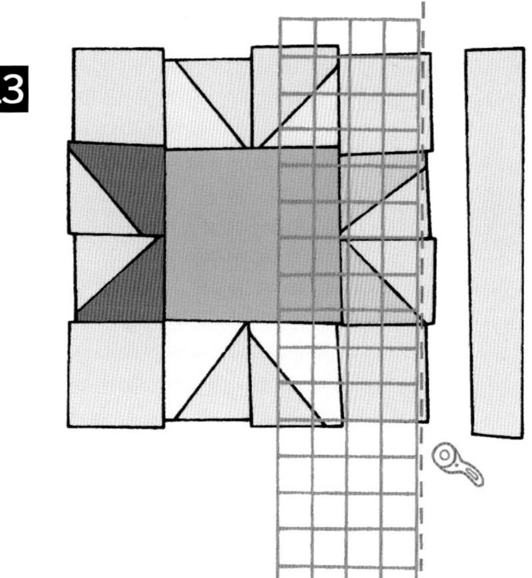


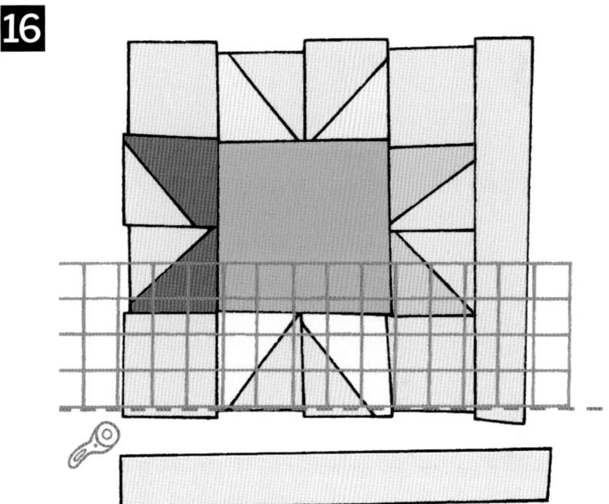


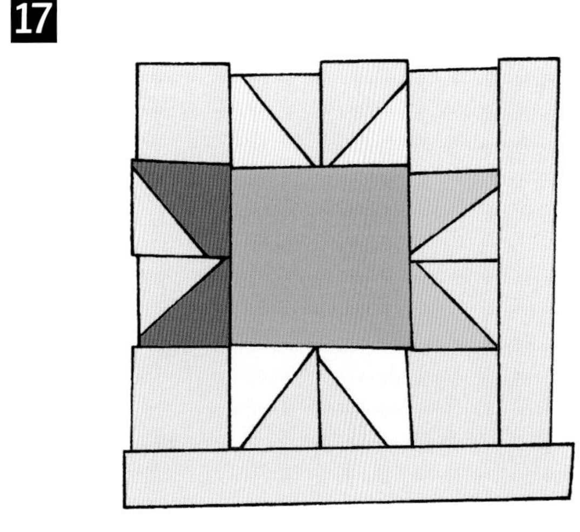

## Assemble—quilt top

**Step 18** Join blocks together in sections of Four-Patches or Two-Patches, using the construction methods on page 19, rather than the traditional technique for sewing rows together. Trim all edges being joined with a straight edge prior to sewing. Press open.

**Step 19** Continue joining segments together non-traditionally until the quilt top is complete. Trim all edges being joined with a straight edge prior to sewing. Press open after every seam sewn.

**Step 20** Add sashing to the top and left sides of the quilt. Cut strips approximately 2in (5cm) wide, and assemble to the width and height of the quilt. Sew right sides together, then press open.

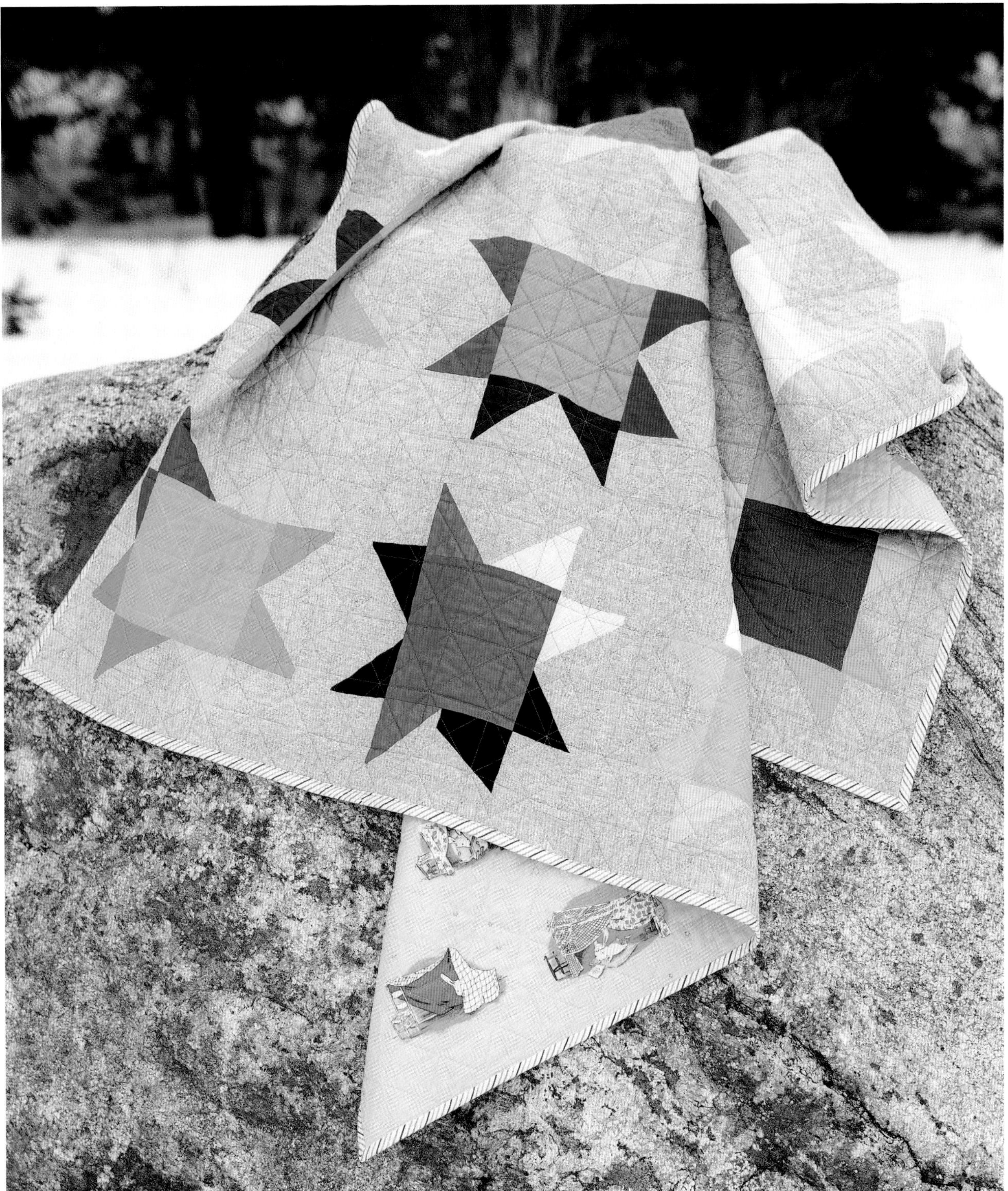

## Finishing the quilt

See notes on quilt finishing, pages 116–122.

The sample quilt is quilted on a domestic machine with an edge-to-edge grid and cross-hatch design and machine binding.

# Project 4: Scrap-bin Cleanout

Do you have a pile of scraps and are uncertain what to do with them? Maybe it is in a box or a bin, maybe it is stashed in the back of your closet or the corner of your room. Regardless of how organized, or disorganized, it is, it's time to grab all those scraps and use them for something creative.

Typically, our scraps do not end up all the same size and shape, so a scrap-bin cleanout is the perfect way to train your brain to puzzle piece together a ruler-cut improv quilt.

Please read through all the instructions for this project before starting. For this quilt you will practice your straight-edge improv cutting and piecing skills, and apply a color harmony or your rainbow.

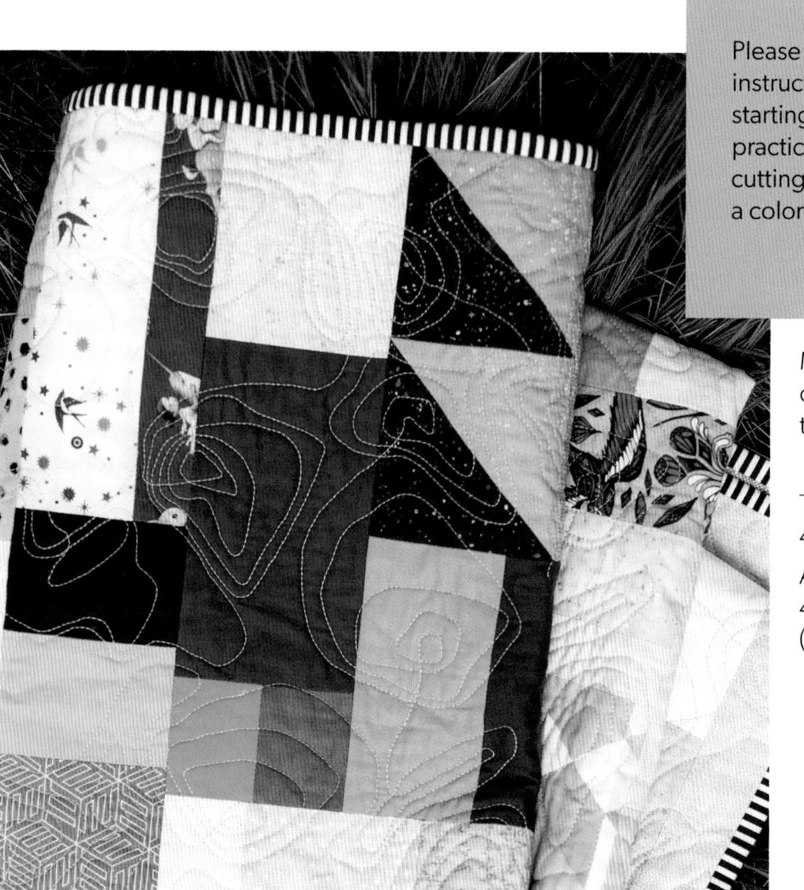

My selected color harmony is split complementary (see page 22), including the colors blue, green, and red-orange.

The finished sample quilt size is 46½ x 57in (118 x 145cm).

Aim to have a finished quilt size around 45 x 60in (114 x 152cm) to 60 x 75in (152cm x 190cm).

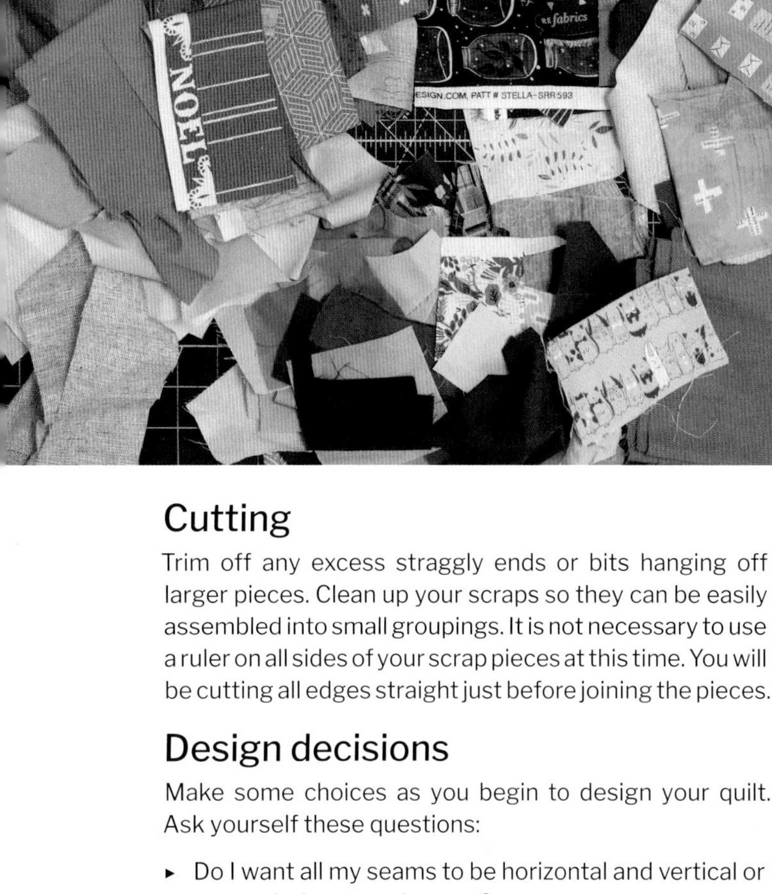


## Sort your scraps

The first thing you want to do is to sort your scraps into color piles. If you have a lot of scraps, you may choose a color harmony and work with only a select number of colors. If you have fewer scraps, you might be working with your rainbow and including all the colors.

Whichever colors you choose to work with, sort all your scraps into appropriate color piles.

## Cutting

Trim off any excess straggly ends or bits hanging off larger pieces. Clean up your scraps so they can be easily assembled into small groupings. It is not necessary to use a ruler on all sides of your scrap pieces at this time. You will be cutting all edges straight just before joining the pieces.

## Design decisions

Make some choices as you begin to design your quilt. Ask yourself these questions:

- Do I want all my seams to be horizontal and vertical or are angled seams okay too?
- Will I include a background fabric or solely use small scraps?
- Is there balance in scrap sizes? Are there areas or color sections that have small scraps that need large pieces added in from stash?
- Is there balance in value? Does each light area or dark area have an opposite light or dark area to balance the overall composition?
- Is there balance in repeating shapes? Design happens best in threes. Intentionally add design elements to your quilt three times.
- Where do I need filler pieces?

## Color play

Once you have your scraps sorted and have a plan for the main design components it's time to play with those colors.

1. Arrange three areas of color blocking using one of the colors you have in your selected color harmony. You can see the three areas of red-orange placed on the design wall. Begin adding scraps to create darker and lighter areas in the composition.

2. Find a color hidden in your stash that you are not drawn to. Look for a color that you left out because it is not your favorite color. Find the complement to that color on your design wall and make room for this new scrap within that color section. By placing the new scrap within its complement's section, you are creating a high-contrast area and adding interest and a place for the viewer's eye to be drawn to. The color-blocked area of lime green contrasts with the nearby grouping of red-orange fabrics.

3. Add several other misplaced scraps into the wrong color sections. These don't need to be colors that you do not like but can be colors that you are already using in the quilt top. Try to work in three to five oddly placed scraps that can balance each other across the entire composition. By deciding on only using horizontal and vertical seams, the HSTs look misplaced and bring interest to the composition. Balance is created by including three areas where darker value HSTs contrast with the surrounding rectangular pieces.

1

2

3

## Assemble—groups

To assemble your pieces into groups you want to eliminate any chance of partial seams or Y-seams (where three edges meet). Arrange the pieces on your design wall into smaller groups that will be sewn together. Make adjacent groups into similar sizes for easy joining when finishing the quilt top. Look for the best places to place your long seam.

Will your quilt be divided into rows, columns, or sections?

See the sample quilt grouping on the right to see how you can think about sectioning your pieces into groups that will be easily pieced into the quilt top.

Start with the two smallest pieces in the group you are working on. Cut a straight edge on the adjacent edges that will be sewn together. Sew right sides together, then press open.

Continue building your grouping by cutting adjacent straight edges each time you will be sewing a piece together.

Add filler pieces as necessary.

## Assemble—quilt top

Just as you avoided partial and Y-seams when assembling your groups, you want to avoid them when assembling your quilt top. When you assembled your groups, you were working to create similar sizes next to each other to make your quilt top assembly easier. Apply filler pieces as needed to make groupings closer to the same size.

Always cut the adjacent edges being sewn together with a straight edge. Sew right sides together, then press open.

## Finishing the quilt

See notes on quilt finishing, pages 116–122.

The sample quilt is finished with a longarm quilted pantograph and hand binding.

*Quilted by Cara Cansler, Sew Colorado Quilting, Westminster, CO.*

# 3

# Improv piecing: Ruler-free

"Always trim adjacent edges with a mirrored contour before sewing them together."

Once you have mastered the ruler-cut improv technique of always sewing a straight edge to a straight edge, you are ready to learn ruler-free improv piecing. There are no big mysteries to learning this technique: instead of sewing adjacent straight edges together, you need to create a mirrored contour.

A mirrored contour is simple even if it sounds complicated. When adjoining adjacent pieces, they must reflect each other's silhouette. Where one piece goes in, the other goes out, and vice versa. The rule to successful ruler-free improv is to always trim pieces with a mirrored contour before sewing them together.

There does not have to be an extreme curvature or wonkiness to your ruler-free improv. Simply cutting freehand will cause the forms of your shapes to soften. You can experiment with more extreme edge shapes, but you will never be able to cut perfectly straight without a ruler. Therefore, I recommend cutting freehand without additional intentional wonkiness.

# BASICS OF RULER-FREE IMPROV PIECING

Just as with ruler-cut improv, you can create basic quilt units with the ruler-free technique. You can use a freehand cutting technique for the common scenarios of Log Cabins, Nine-Patch, and stripes. In addition, you can look at triangles and diagonal cuts with a different eye when cutting ruler-free. For now we will not be addressing more extreme curves like quarter circles or half-arc circles. Those will be covered in chapter 4 (pages 82–99).

## Triangles and diagonal cuts

Unlike in ruler-cut improv, where I like to cut each straight diagonal individually, when cutting without a ruler it is easier to cut pairs of triangles together.

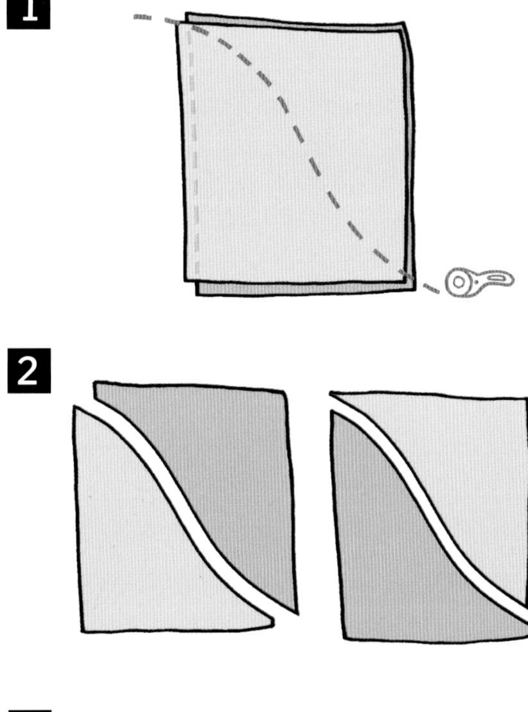


**Step 1** Stack two different fabrics right sides up and then make your ruler-free diagonal cut. You are guaranteed a successful mirrored contour. This is similar to how you can make paired HSTs but you cut before you sew for this improv method.

**Step 2** Switch the fabrics around to make pairs of the opposite fabrics. Remember to keep them right sides up to maintain the mirrored contour.

**Step 3** Sew the pairs right sides together along the mirrored contour edge.

## Cabins, steps, and stripes—otherwise straight edges

Ruler-free Log Cabins use the same basic principles as for ruler-cut improv. Instead of cutting a straight edge on the adjacent edges to be sewn together, slightly overlap the edges you are going to join and use the top edge as a guide to cut the lower piece. This will create a mirrored contour.

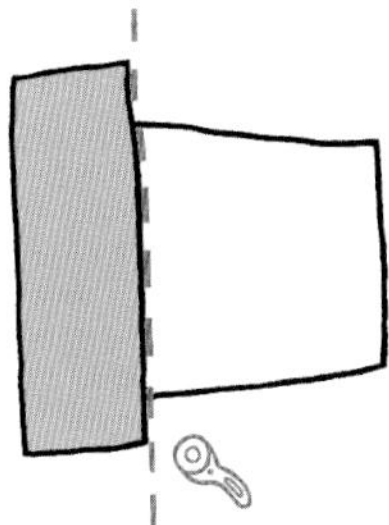

**Step 1** Begin with the center, right side up, and overlap a single piece approximately ⅛in (3mm). Trim the center piece to a mirrored contour using the top edge that is overlapping the center as your guide. Sew right sides together. Press open.

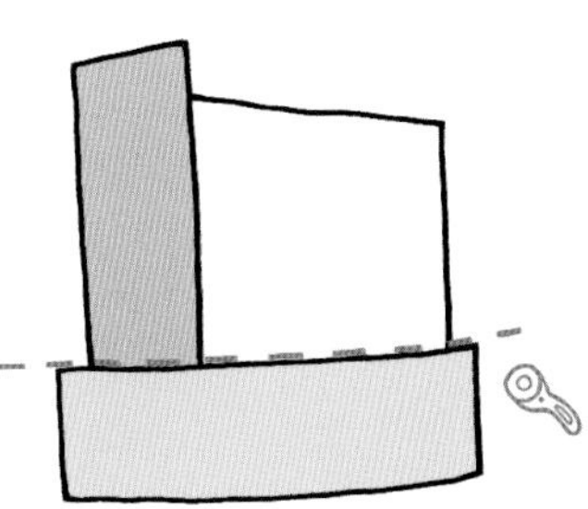

**Step 2** Working around the center, place another piece, overlapping approximately ⅛in (3mm) right side up. Trim the lower pieces to a mirrored contour using the top edge of the new overlapping piece as your guide. Sew right sides together. Press open.

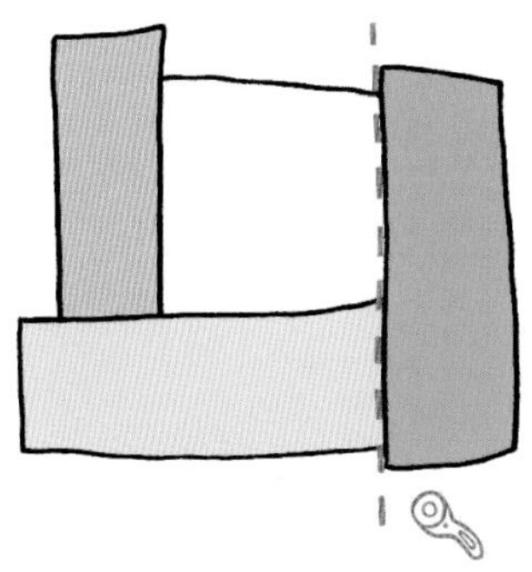

**Step 3** Add another piece to the next side. Overlap approximately ⅛in (3mm), right side up. Trim using the edge of the upper piece as your guide to create the mirrored contour. Sew right sides together. Press open.

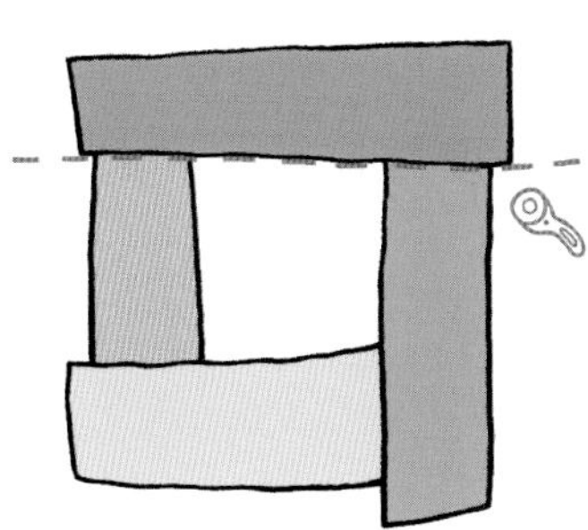

**Step 4** Continue adding pieces around the block using the edge of the new piece to trim against to create the mirrored contour. Sew right sides together. Press open.

**Step 5** Remember that for a flat block you must use an overlapping piece to create the mirrored contour edges before you sew.

**Step 6** Continue repeating the mirrored-contour trimming, and adding pieces until your Log Cabin has grown to the desired size.

## Piecing ruler-free improv segments together

When joining segments with ruler-free improv you will approach it the same way you approach "otherwise straight edges" (see previous page). Place the blocks to be joined together next to each other, right sides up, and slightly overlapping about ⅛in (3mm). Use the block on top as a guide to create your mirrored contour.

## Notes on joining jagged edges

When overlapping two segments that will be sewn together to create a mirrored contour, you may come across a scenario when you have jagged edges on both pieces. There are two ways to tackle this challenge.

You can pre-trim one of the pieces along the side that will be used to overlap the other segment. You can then easily use the new edge to create the mirrored contour. You will be trimming off all the jagged edges from the piece below when the mirrored contour is cut.

Or, you can overlap the segments before trimming either jagged edge. Instead of using the top piece as a guide for the new mirrored contour edge, cut ruler-free halfway between the top piece edge and the bottom piece edge. Remove the trimmings from the pieces to reveal the mirrored contour.

# Project 5: Squash Blossom

Your ruler-free cutting does not need to be chaotic or overly curvy. You can see that simply cutting without a straight edge gives a softer, more playful feeling to this traditional block.

Use a traditional Squash Blossom block and layout for this project, which is constructed from HSTs and strips.

Please read through all the instructions for this project before starting. You will use a traditional block and layout to practice your ruler-free improv cutting and piecing skills, and apply a color harmony.

## REQUIREMENTS

The sample uses 29 unique fabrics. Each fabric is included once or twice as an approximately 10in (25.5cm) square. You will need a total of 48 approximately 10in (25.5cm) squares.

My selected color harmony is split analogous (see page 23), including the colors yellow-green, yellow-orange, red-orange, and red-violet.

The finished sample quilt size is 53 x 57½in (135 x 146cm).

Aim for a finished quilt of a similar size.

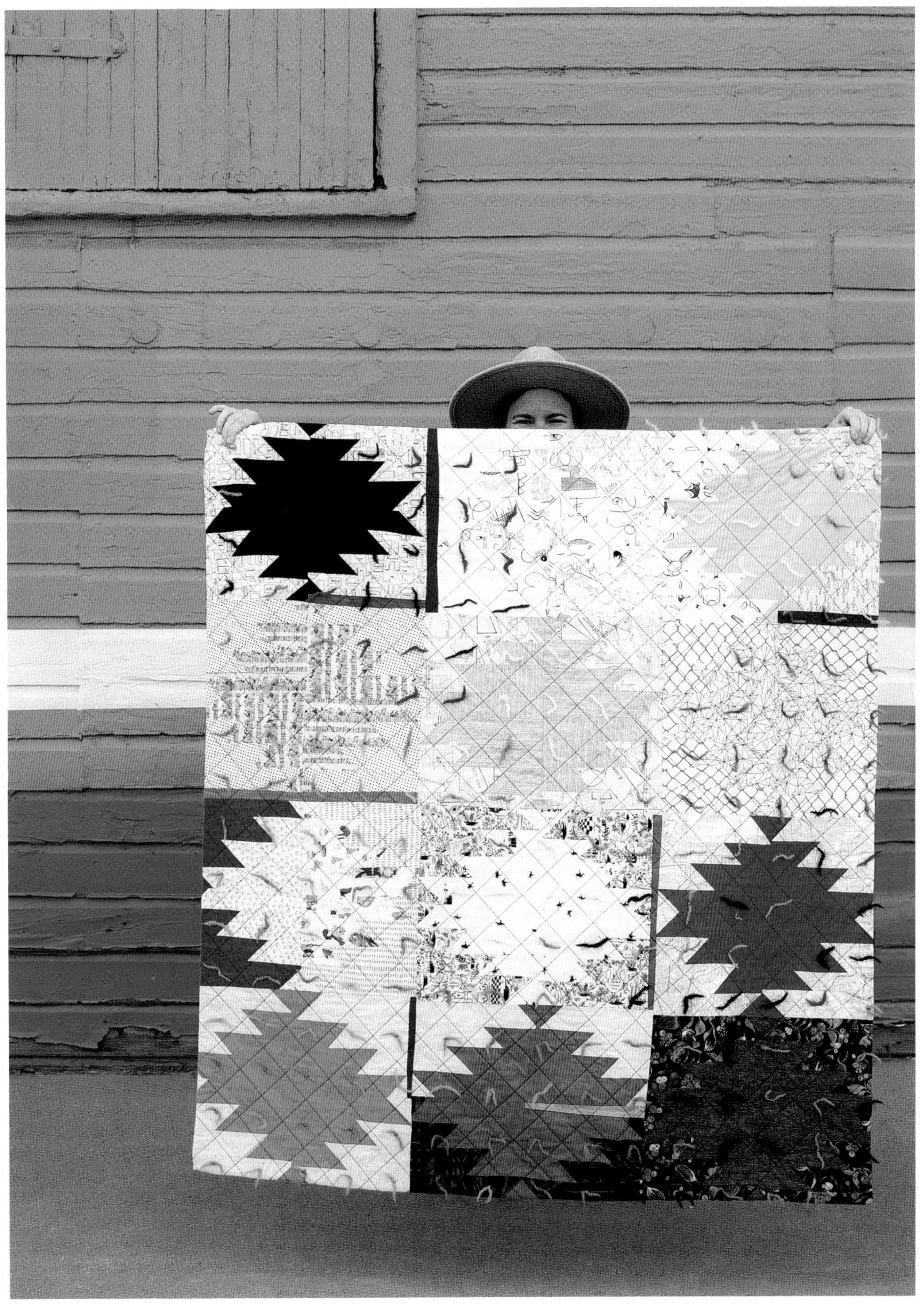

## Color sketch

Select the color harmony you will use for your project. Use any of the color harmonies discussed in chapter 1 or use your rainbow colors determined in project 2. Using colored pencils to represent your fabric colors, illustrate a coloring sheet of the Squash Blossom quilt to determine each color location (on page 126).

## Cutting

Using your coloring sheet to identify color placement, in total:

- Cut 48 squares using the ruler-free technique and your cutting mat measurement markings to approximately 10 x 10in (25.5 x 25.5cm) (refer to "Improve your improv" on page 18). For most fabrics, cut 2 squares from each.

## Design wall

Arrange the squares on your design wall, pairing each fabric with a contrasting background fabric (as I've done on the right). The pairs—two squares from each fabric—will create a single Squash Blossom block. Some blocks may include more than two fabrics. All blocks will consist of four approximately 10in (25.5cm) squares.

## Assemble—blocks

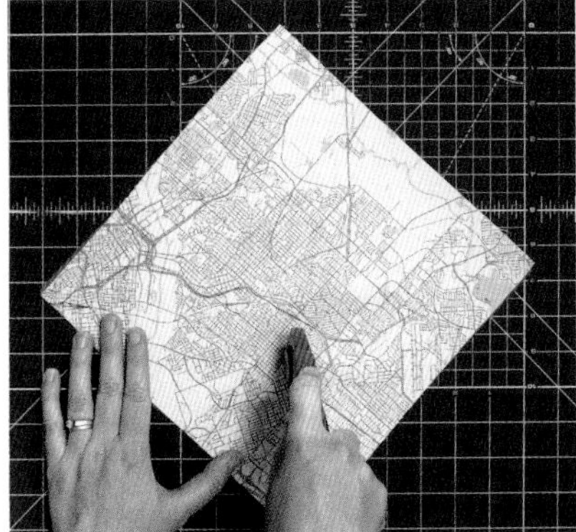

**Step 1** Stack one pair of fabric squares, both face-up. Cut diagonally from corner to corner through both layers. Repeat to cut a second matching pair of squares.

**Step 2** Keeping the cut triangles face-up, pair each background triangle with its color triangle, maintaining the mirrored contour created by the diagonal cut.

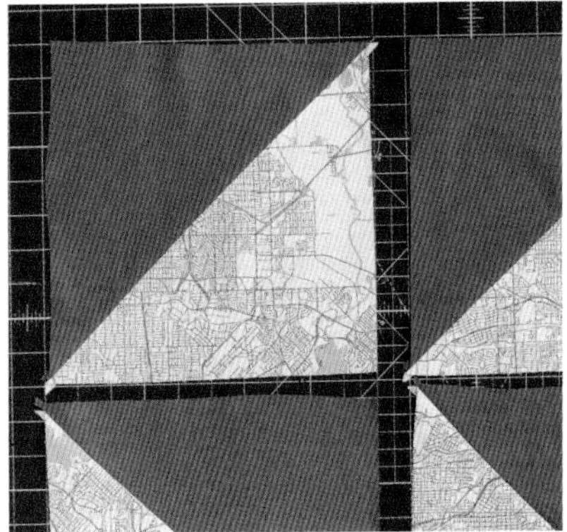

**Step 3** Sew pairs right sides together along the mirrored contour diagonal using a ¼in (5mm) seam allowance. Press open.

**Step 4** Repeat with all the fabric pairs to create HSTs.

**Step 5** For each block, arrange 2 HSTs so that the seam is diagonally bottom left to top right and 2 HSTs so that the seam is diagonally top left to bottom right. Cut ruler-free, vertically through the approximate center of each HST.

**Step 6** Cut ruler-free, vertically through each half HST dividing all HSTs into four vertical strips.

**Step 7** Rearrange the strips to create stepped segments in groups of four, as shown.

**Step 8** Trim the strips by overlapping adjacent strips approximately ⅛in (3mm) and using the top strip as a guide to cut a mirrored contour. Sew the right sides together. Press open. Continue adding each strip with the overlapping mirrored-contour trimming method for the remaining strips in the group of four. Repeat for each group of four strips.

**Step 9** Arrange the assembled strip panels to create the Squash Blossom block.

**Step 10** Complete the block by sewing quadrant panels (blocks of 4 strips) right sides together using the ruler-free mirrored-contour technique. Use filler strips as needed. Press open.

You can see how I've added filler strips below, within the blocks and between them as needed.

## Assemble—quilt top

**Step 11** Arrange blocks according to your Squash Blossom coloring sheet.

**Step 12** Join blocks together in sections of Four-Patches or Two-Patches. Avoid using traditional construction methods of sewing rows together (see page 19, Avoiding a striped quilt for more on this). Trim all edges being joined using the mirrored-contour technique prior to sewing. Press open after every seam sewn.

**Step 13** Continue joining segments together non-traditionally until the quilt top is complete. Trim all edges being joined using the mirrored-contour technique prior to sewing. Press open after every seam sewn.

## Finishing the quilt

See notes on quilt finishing, pages 116–122.

The sample quilt is quilted on a domestic machine with an edge-to-edge, on-point grid design and hand tied with yarn. The edge is finished with a facing.

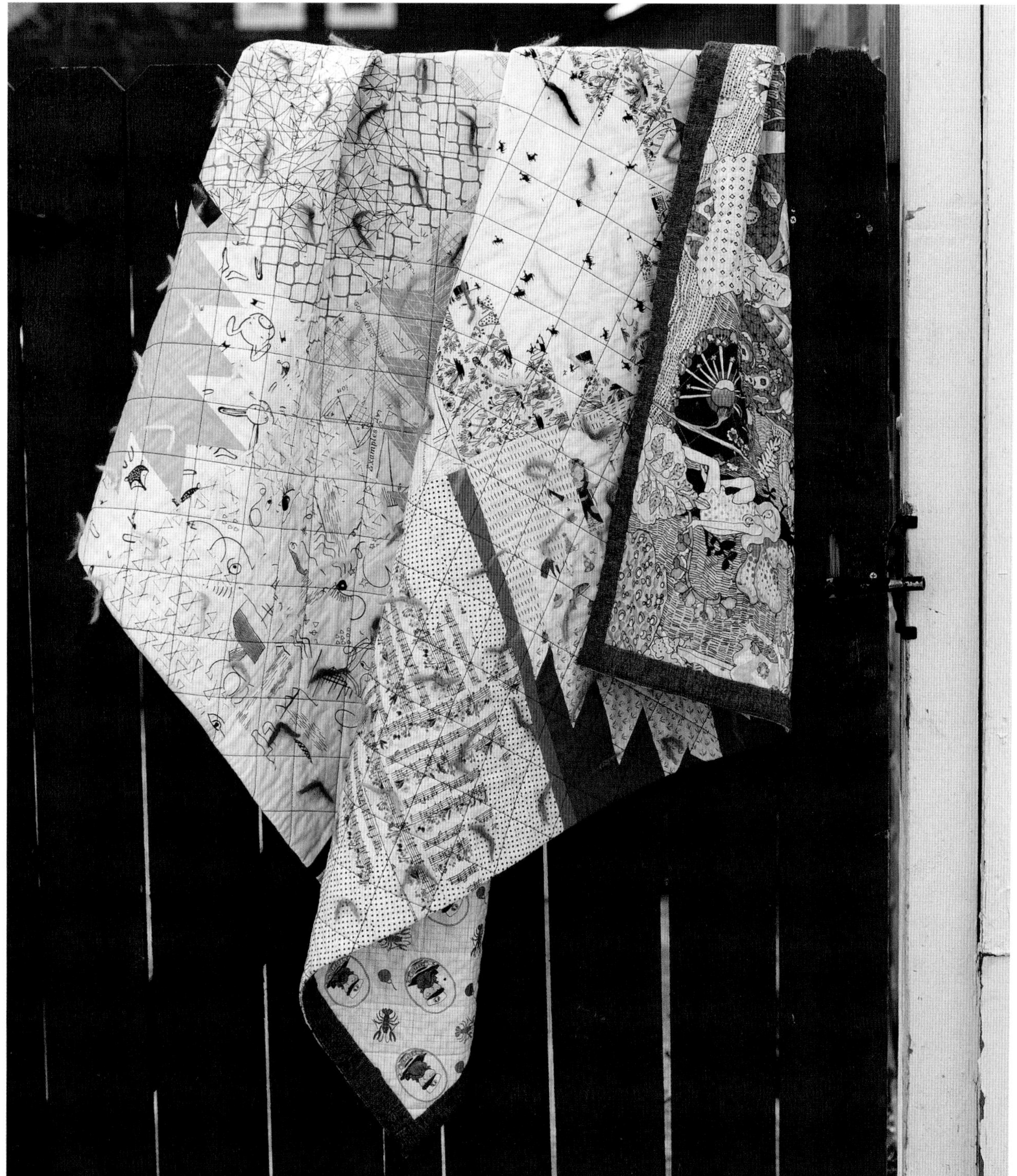

# Project 6: Large Piecing

For this project you will need to trust your gut and listen to the fabric as you place pieces on the design wall. This is the first project dabbling in intuitive improv design. By using larger pieces, you have an opportunity to reflect on the feeling of the quilt without getting bogged down by intricate piecing or complicated technical skills.

Please read through all the instructions for this project before starting. You will be practicing ruler-free cutting and piecing and making improv design decisions. In addition to your selected color harmony and chosen fabrics, make sure to select one fabric that stands out from the rest. If you are using all solids, select a print; if you are using all warm colors, select a cool color, and so on.

My selected color harmony is split complementary (see page 22), including the colors green, red, yellow-green, and red-violet.

The finished sample quilt is 55 x 65in (140 x 165cm).
Aim to have a finished quilt around 50 x 60in (127 x 152cm) to 65 x 70in (165 x 178cm).

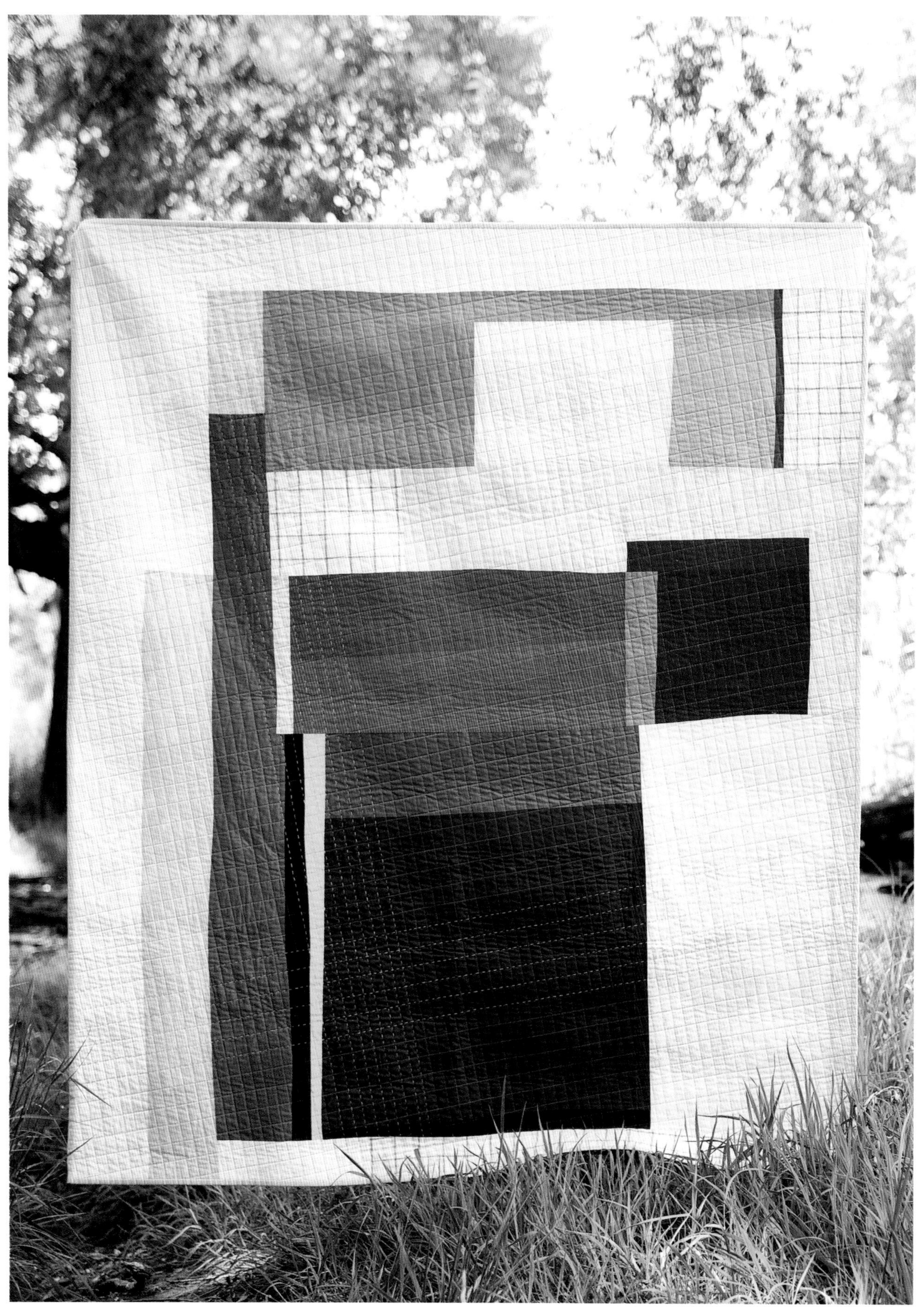

## Design-wall play

To begin your large piecing design, select one large cut of fabric, approximately the size of a fat quarter, and use your ruler-free cutting technique to soften the edges. Place your first piece on the wall.

Continue to add more large pieces to create movement or tension between the colors. Aim for most pieces to be sized at least 6 x 10in (15 x 25.5cm) or larger.

Ask yourself these design questions:

- Is there balance in piece sizes? Are there areas or color sections that need smaller pieces added? Adding in sections of smaller pieces, sized down to 4 x 4in (10 x 10cm) or skinny strips as narrow as 1–2in (2.5–5cm) wide will give weight to the largest pieces. Add in only a few purposeful smaller pieces and trust that when assembling sections of the quilt you will need some filler pieces that will also be at a smaller scale. Create balance in piece sizes by including color-blocked areas like the red-violet or red areas of the sample quilt. These areas help the darkest green area to not become a void in the design but a focal point.
- Is there balance in value? Does each light area or dark area have an opposite light or dark area to balance the overall composition? Even the smallest bit of dark inserted away from the main dark area will help to even out the layout of the quilt design. In the sample, the small strip of dark in the upper right of the quilt supports the larger dark areas in the lower center.
- Is there balance in repeating shapes? Design happens best in threes: intentionally add design elements to your quilt three times.

Top assembly pieces arranged into groups.

You can use the same bold or contrasting fabric choices multiple times within the quilt design. Balance can be achieved by making high-contrast areas with light and dark fabrics used together or by using a bold fabric in a quilt of muted colors. In the sample quilt, a black and white printed grid fabric is used as a contrast to the bold, solid-color fabrics. It appears three times across the composition of the quilt.

After adding in smaller sections or pieces to help with balance, you may have drifted away from larger cuts of fabric. Return to adding larger pieces to the design. Step back and evaluate what your design is missing. If you have not yet added in a high-contrast or bold area to draw the eye, create that element at this stage.

## Assemble—quilt top

Using the ruler-free, mirrored-contour method, begin assembling sections of your quilt top.

- Will your quilt be divided into rows, columns, or groups? Think about sectioning your pieces into groups that will be easily pieced into the quilt top. You want to eliminate chances of partial seams or Y-seams. Arrange pieces on your design wall into smaller sections to be sewn together (an illustration of the sample quilt groups is shown opposite). Make adjacent sections into similar sizes for easier joining. Look ahead for the best places to put your longest seams.
- How will you assemble the quilt sections? Start with the two smallest pieces in the group you are working on. Make sure to overlap the adjacent edges that will be sewn together and trim with the ruler-free technique to create a mirrored contour. Trim jagged edges off larger segments before cutting the mirror contour if needed. Sew right sides together, then press open.
- Are there areas that need filler pieces? Is it best to trim down, add a contrasting filler, or add a blending filler? Should you introduce a new fabric or reuse something already in the design? Even a small filler piece can make an impact on the overall quilt design. Look at the royal blue strip to the right of the darkest, largest green piece. Although this filler is subtle in value by still being dark, it adds an interesting contrast by including a new color not in the original color harmony selected, giving a little extra character to the quilt.

Balance is created by having opposing dark areas in the quilt, a mix of very large and some smaller pieces, and using the printed grid fabric in three areas.

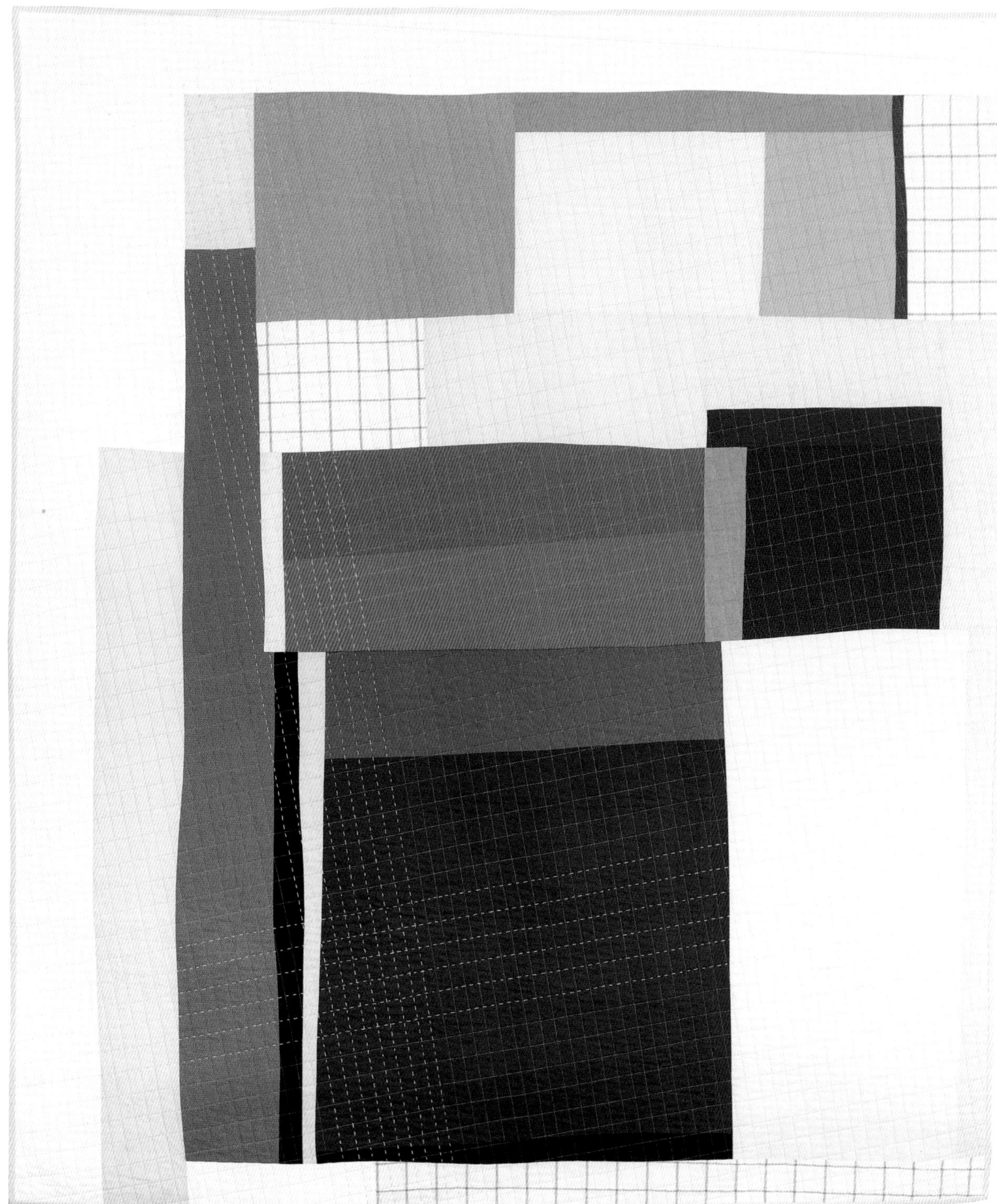

## Finishing the quilt

See notes on quilt finishing, pages 116–122.

The sample quilt is quilted on a domestic machine with an edge-to-edge, skewed grid design and hand-quilted accents. The binding is sewn by hand.

# 4

# Advanced improv piecing: Curves

After working through the first six projects, you will have learned skills for traditional angled quilt shapes like squares, rectangles, and triangles using both ruler-cut and ruler-free improv piecing techniques.

Now you can explore more advanced shapes. Curves are notoriously tricky quilt shapes that typically require precision, possibly a lot of pins or glue, and trimming for accuracy. Here, however, you're in luck, because improv curves are relatively forgiving.

Keep in mind the secret to ruler-free improv—the mirrored contour—and you will be successful in making improv curves. If you are a beginner at sewing curves, keep them shallow and the construction will be less complicated. More experienced quilters can choose deeper curves. Never shy away from dividing your curve into easier-to-sew segments to reach the result you desire.

There are several types of curves or curved units you may encounter while improv quilting. Time to dive in!

# EXPLORING CURVED IMPROV

## Quarter circle

As when cutting HSTs for ruler-free improv, stacking your selected fabrics right sides up and cutting through both layers to make your mirrored contour is my favorite approach. The steeper your freehand quarter circle cut is, the harder it will be to sew. As a beginner, make your curved cut a bit flatter.

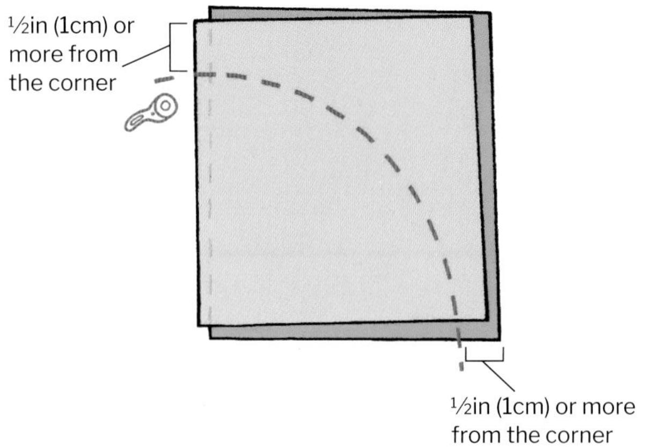


**Step 1** Stack your fabrics right-side up and cut your curve approximately ½in (1cm) or more from opposite corners.

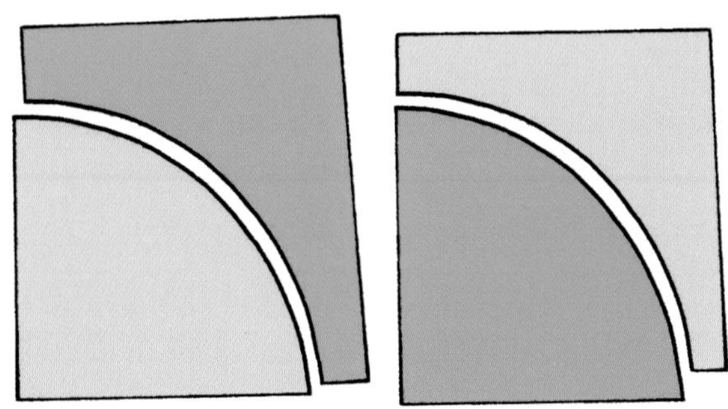

**Step 2** Unstack the shapes and switch the pieces to match with their mirrored contour. This will give you two opposite-colored quarter-circle units.

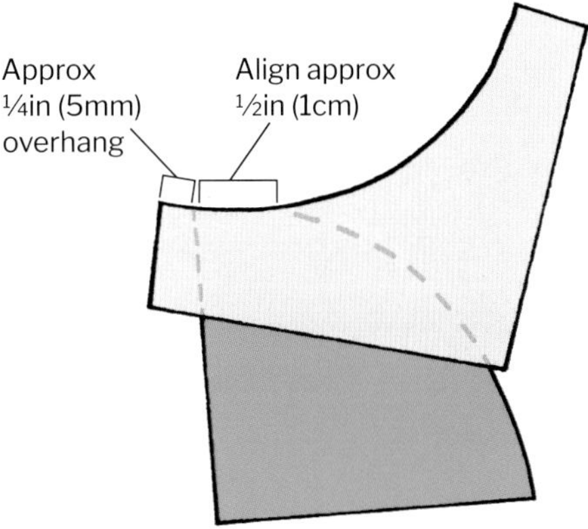


**Step 3** Do not line up the edges. The edge of the concave piece (the wrong side of the light green piece) should overhang the edge of the convex piece (dark green) by approximately ¼in (5mm) to allow for the seam allowance. With right sides together, align approximately ½in (2.5cm) of the edges of the pieces.

**Step 4** Begin sewing and ease around the curve, aligning edges as you sew. Take care not to stretch the fabrics on the bias as you sew the seam. The unit will also overhang slightly on the other end when you finish sewing. Pins are not necessary as there is plenty of flexibility to trim after your unit is sewn. Press open.

## Half-circle arc

As with HSTs and quarter circles, stack your fabrics to cut ruler-free and create your mirrored contour. And again, because you are not using a template, the edges of the curved pieces will not align. Start by matching the center and work your way to the edges using pins or glue to secure your pieces together before sewing. This is one of the few times in improv that I use pins.

Assembly of half-circle arcs is covered in depth in project 8, pages 92–96.

## Wedge arc

A precaution that you have taken when making any kind of improv stripe panel was to be sure to align your wedge shapes with alternating wide ends to avoid creating an arc. In the instance of creating an intentional arc, you want to purposefully align all your wedge shapes in the same orientation. Align your wedges with the wide ends on the same side and your arc will form naturally.

In traditional piecing we see a wedge arc in blocks like a Double Wedding Ring or a Pickle Dish. More complicated wedge arcs can occur in a New York Beauty block.

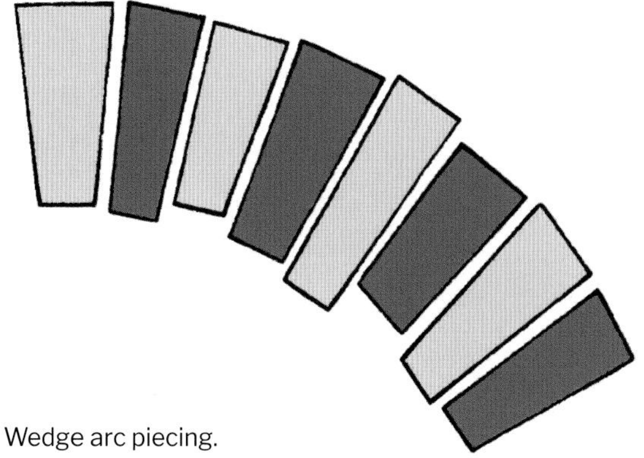

Wedge arc piecing.

# Project 7: Wagon Wheel

A traditional Wagon Wheel block includes the processes of both creating wedge arcs and piecing a quarter circle. Practice feeling uncomfortable with the imperfections of the wedge sizes and the mismatched quarter circle shapes within each block. You will also work on sashing and joining blocks with the ruler-free technique.

Please read through all the instructions for this project before starting. This quilt uses a traditional Wagon Wheel block and layout so you can practice your advanced curves improv skills using quarter circles and wedge arcs. Use a ruler-free improv technique for non-curved components.

My selected color harmony is analogous (see page 23), including the colors red, red-violet, and violet-red with limited contrasting accents in yellow-orange and blue-green. There is a coloring sheet on page 127 if you wish to plan your color harmony.

The finished sample quilt is 63 x 65½in (160 x 166cm).

Aim for a finished quilt of a similar size.

## Assemble—wedge arcs

**Step 1** Cut 3 rectangles from each background and wedge accent fabric approximately 3½ x 8in (9 x 20.5cm).

**Step 2** Cut approximately 6 wedges from each rectangle.

**Step 3** Align wedge shapes, alternating fabrics and keeping the wide ends towards the same side to create an arc. For each block create four quarter-circle arcs.

**Step 4** Sew the wedges into arcs, right sides together, then press open.

## Assemble—quarter circles

**Step 5** Align a wedge arc right side up on the background fabric. Cut along the outer edge to create a mirrored contour. Trim the background surround to approximately 10½ x 10½in (26.5 x 26.5cm). Reserve the inner quarter circle for step 7.

**Step 6** Sew the wedge arc to the background surround, right sides together. Press open.

**Step 7** Place the wedge arc + background surround right side up on inner quarter circle. Cut along the inner edge to create a mirrored contour. Discard the extra fabric.

**Step 8** Sew the wedge arc and attached background surround to the inner quarter circle. Press open.

**Step 9** Ruler-free trim excess fabric to "square up" the quarter circle unit to approximately 10 x 10in (25.5 x 25.5cm).

**Step 10** Repeat for each quadrant.

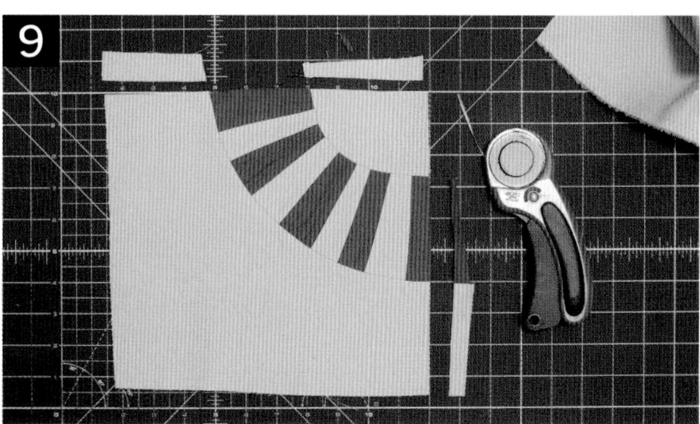

## Assemble—Wagon Wheels

**Step 11** Cut 4 rectangles from sashing accent fabric, each approximately 2½ x 10in (6 x 25.5cm). Cut center square approximately 2½ x 2½in ( 6.5 x 6.5cm).

**Step 12** Using the ruler-free mirrored contour technique (see page 65), assemble your Wagon Wheel block into columns: quarter circle + sashing + quarter circle; sashing + center square + sashing; quarter circle + sashing + quarter circle. Press open. Sew columns right sides together using the ruler-free mirrored-contour technique. Press open.

**Step 13** Ruler-free trim any jagged edges off to prepare the block for sashing. Repeat all assembly instructions to create 9 Wagon Wheel blocks.

## Assemble—quilt top

**Step 14** Cut 16 approximately 2½ x 2½in (6.5 x 6.5cm) cornerstones and 24 approximately 2½in x 22in (6.5cm x 56cm) sashing strips. Attach the sashing and cornerstones to the bottom and right edges of each Wagon Wheel block using the ruler-free mirrored-contour technique. Use the Nine-Patch segments assembly method (see page 19) to assemble the quilt top. Attach the remaining sashing and cornerstones to the top and left edges of the quilt top using the ruler-free mirrored-contour technique.

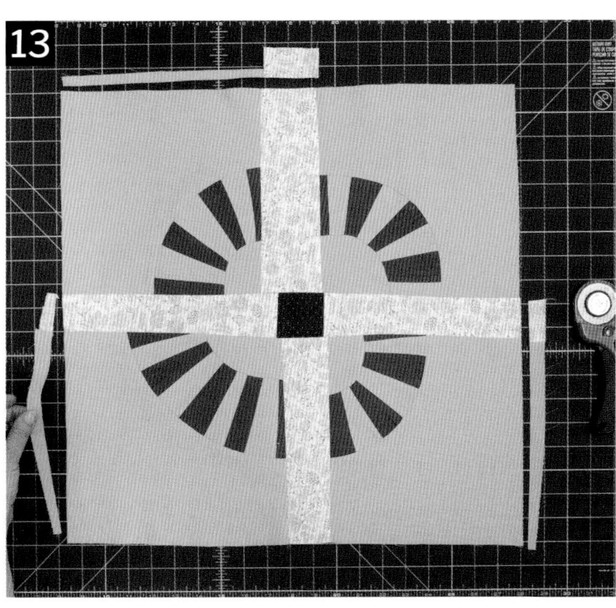

## Finishing the quilt

See notes on quilt finishing, pages 116–122.

The sample quilt is finished with a longarm quilted pantograph and machine binding.

*Quilted by Cara Cansler, Sew Colorado Quilting, Westminster, CO.*

# Project 8: Rainbow Arcs

Creating a rainbow arc uses a half-circle arc piecing technique. A half-circle arc is the one place in improv quilting where I like to use pins (as shown on page 94, step 5). Alternatively, you could choose to use glue, clips, or nothing at all to secure your arcs before sewing. This project is also a great time to practice adding filler. Simple, solid color chunks give the eye a place to rest, while more advanced wonky stars used as filler add to the fun and whimsy of this quilt.

Please read through all the instructions for this project before starting. For this quilt you will practice advanced curves improv skills using half-circle arcs. Apply a new color harmony or version of your rainbow to each arc. It is easiest to work with fat quarters or yardage of each color.

I have selected to use my rainbow colors for this project. Each rainbow arc contains a unique color harmony group.

The finished sample quilt size is 53½ x 64in (136 x 162.5cm).

Aim for a finished quilt size around 50 x 60in (127 x 152cm) to 65 x 70in (165 x 178cm).

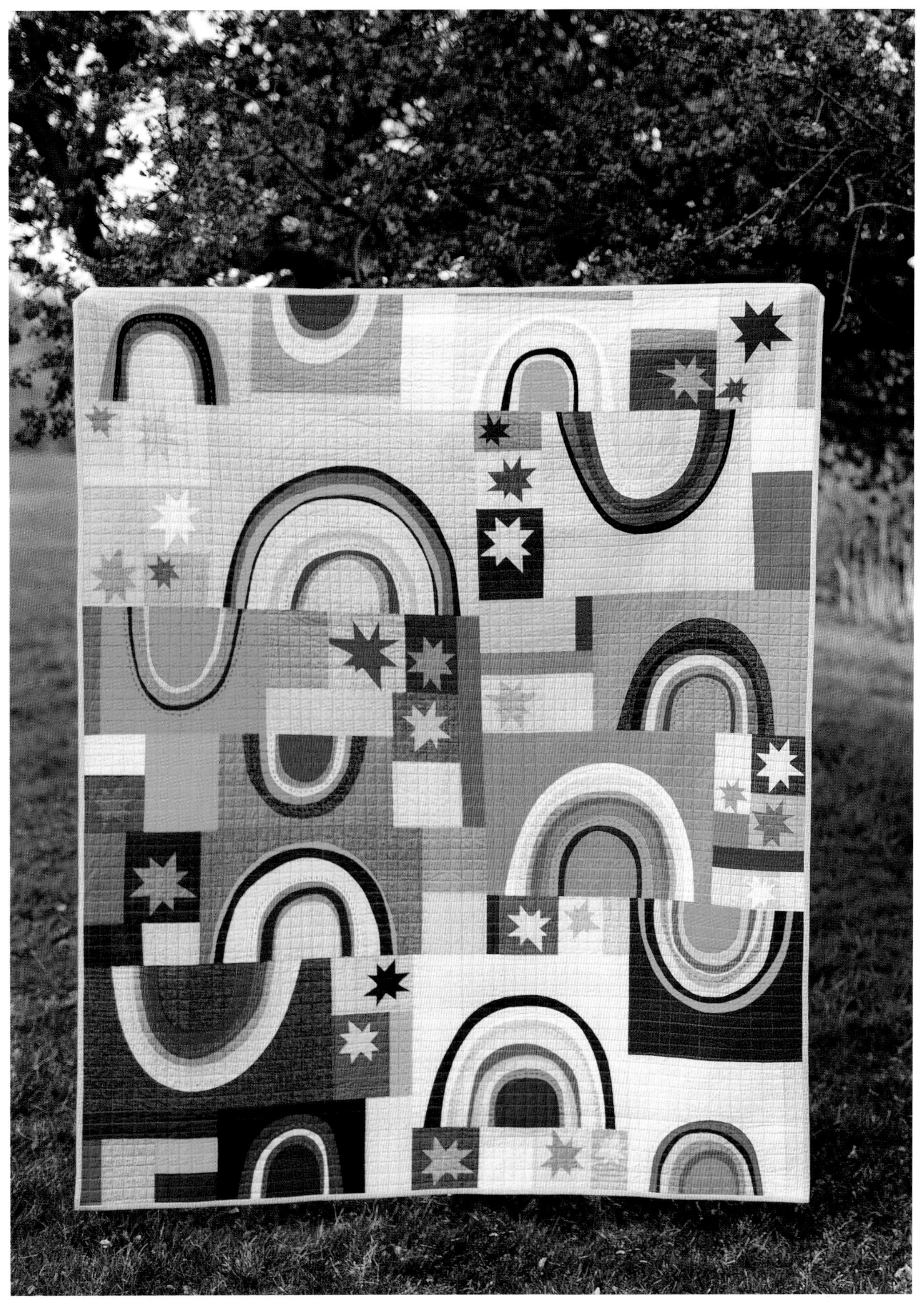

## Color play

Select 4 or 5 color harmonies (see pages 22–26) and group fabrics together to apply to your arcs. Include 3–12 fabrics in each group.

Arrange each group of fabrics in either color or value gradient order.

## Assemble—half-circle arcs

**Step 1** Choose a background fabric for a single group of fabrics. Cut a square approximately 6 x 6in (15 x 15cm) for the central background section.

**Step 2** With right sides facing up on both fabrics, layer the background center on top of the first rainbow arc color. Cut a half-circle arc ruler-free, creating a mirrored contour between the background fabric and the first arc fabric. Remove the first arc fabric from underneath the background fabric and reserve for future rainbow arcs.

**Step 3** Cut a larger half-circle arc, ruler-free from the first arc fabric. Keep in mind you will lose ½in (1cm) of arc width in the seam allowances. I recommend cutting any arcs at least ¾in (2cm) wide.

**Step 4** Align the center point of each arc, then flip the larger arc down, right sides together, onto the background fabric, keeping the centers aligned. Pin at the center.

**Step 5** Working from the center point, continue outwards, aligning the fabric edges, right sides together and pinning. Repeat for the second side.

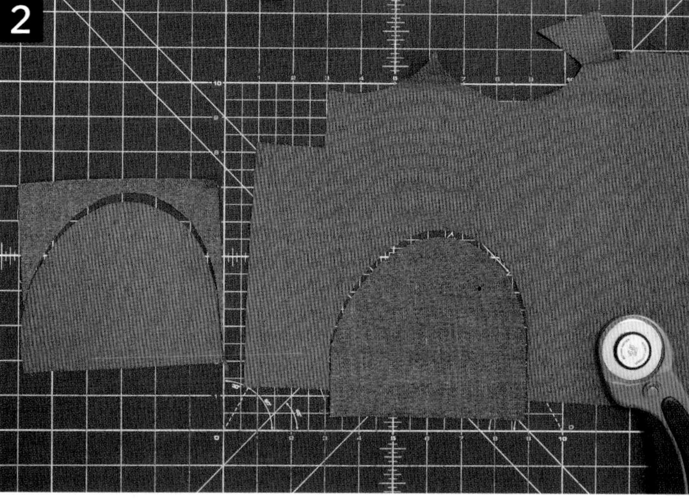


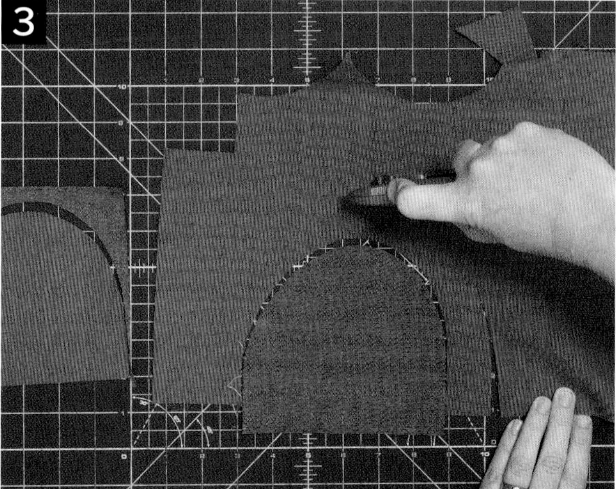

**Step 6** Sew right sides together along the pinned edge, using a scant ¼in (5mm) seam allowance. Ease the fabric through the machine to avoid pleats and puckers.

**Step 7** Using a steamy iron and/or a spray bottle of water, begin pressing the seam open from the center point, working outward to the edges. Repeat for the second side. Take care not to stretch the fabric while pressing.

**Step 8** Select the next arc fabric. Align the sewn arc(s) and center background fabric right sides up on the next arc fabric. Using the outer edge of the previous arc, cut a mirrored contour into the next arc fabric. Remove the next arc fabric from below the sewn arc(s) and center background fabric and reserve for future rainbow arcs.

**Step 9** Cut a larger half-circle arc ruler-free from the next arc fabric. Correct any dipped or wobbly areas by making the new arc wider or skinnier in areas as needed.

**Step 10** Pin, sew, and press as directed in steps 4–7.

**Step 11** Continue selecting fabric and cutting as directed in steps 8–9, and then pinning, sewing arcs, and pressing as directed in steps 4–7, until the rainbow-arc color grouping is complete.

**Step 12** Select a background fabric. Place the rainbow arcs section on top of the background fabric, right sides up. Using the outer edge of the last arc, cut a mirrored contour into the background fabric. Remove the background fabric from below the rainbow arcs section and reserve for future rainbow arcs. Trim the background fabric to a manageable block size as needed.

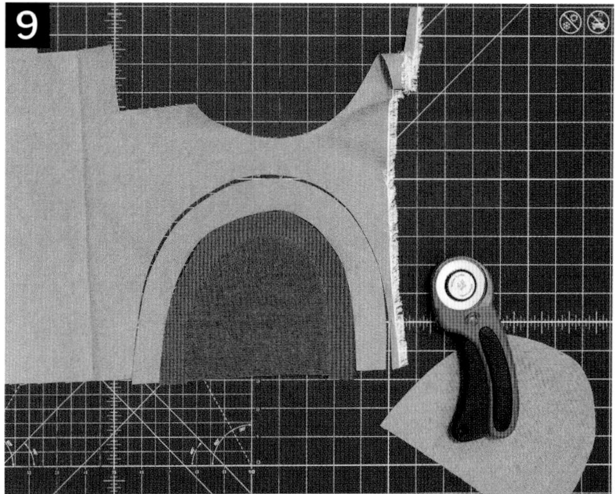

9

12

**Step 13** Align the center point of the arc section with the center point of the background arc edge. Flip the background arc right sides together onto the rainbow arc section, keeping the centers aligned. Pin at the center.

**Step 14** Working from the center point, continue outwards, aligning the fabric edges right sides together and pinning. Repeat for the second side.

**Step 15** Sew right sides together along the pinned edge using a scant ¼in (5mm) seam allowance. Ease, do not stretch, the fabric through the machine to avoid pleats and puckers.

**Step 16** Using a steamy iron and/or a spray bottle of water, begin pressing the seam open from the center point and work out to the edges. Repeat for the second side. Take care not to stretch the fabric while pressing.

**Step 17** Trim the bottom edge of the rainbow arc.

**Step 18** Using the arc scraps reserved for future rainbow arcs, create new color harmonies and repeat the half-circle arc assembly process, steps 1–17. Make approximately 10–15 rainbow arcs for your quilt top.

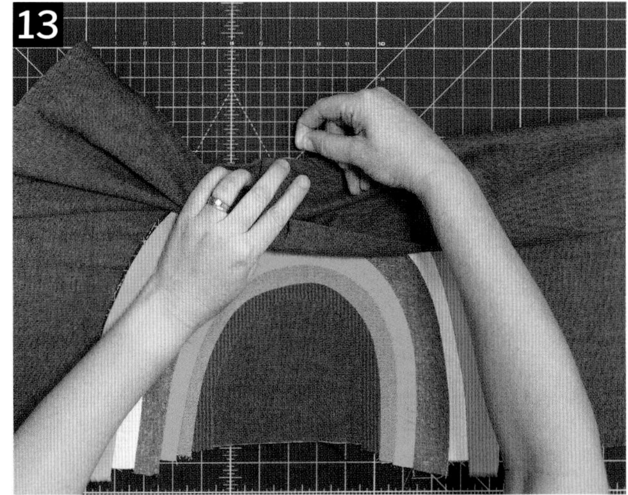


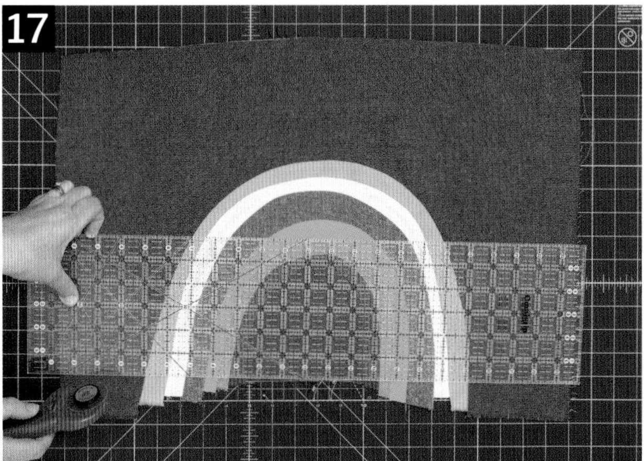

## Assemble—quilt top

**Step 19** Add filler pieces between your rainbow arcs. Using a color harmony or rainbow gradient, arrange the rainbow-arc units based on the background fabrics of each rainbow arc.

### Tip

When planning your filler pieces, use bits of scrap fabric on your design wall to identify where certain colors will be on the quilt top. Fill in with appropriately sized pieces as you identify the best color for the area.

## *Advanced filler*

Consider adding more detail by using another unit or quilt block as filler. The sample quilt uses wonky star blocks as filler. You could also use units like Flying Geese, HSTs, or HRTs. Advanced filler adds more interest to the quilt by allowing even more fabrics and colors to be incorporated into the color gradient.

## Finishing the quilt

See notes on quilt finishing, pages 116–122.

The sample quilt is quilted on a domestic machine with an edge-to-edge grid design and hand-quilted accents. The binding is sewn by hand.

# 5

# Putting it all together: Your improv voice

Now that you have the tools and skills to create colorful improv quilts, where do you come up with ideas? You do not have to feature everything—pick and choose the elements you want to include in your design and focus on those things. You may need to take it back to basics and make a two-color quilt to showcase improv piecing. Keeping it simple with basic patchwork to highlight color placement in your quilt may also be the right choice for you. Now is the time to unlock your improv expression!

It doesn't have to be scary. You can stick to traditional quilt shapes and still create unique improv quilts. Look back to project 6 (page 76), large piecing, and incorporate areas that do not have intricate piecing. Use a favorite traditional block as in projects 1, 3, 5, or 7 (pages 28, 48, 68, and 86) and apply colors in a gradient. Focus on color blocking as in projects 2 or 4 (pages 34 and 56), or move through gradients within a color harmony or your rainbow like in project 8 (page 92). By smashing together your favorite quilt shapes, your favorite improv techniques, and applying color thoughtfully, you can create your own voice.

To get you started on combining techniques and form for your own improv voice, projects 9 and 10 (pages 104 and 11) are prompts to jumpstart your improv designs.

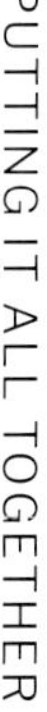

# CREATING YOUR OWN QUILT

Even though I love a good maximalist quilt, I suggest selecting only three things to prioritize in your initial improv quilt designs. As you get more confident and familiar with your own improv voice you can incorporate more design elements into your compositions.

Think about these things as you begin:

**Color selection**
Which colors will you choose? Will you stick to a color harmony? Do you need to include some additional colors beyond sticking to a predefined harmony?

**Color application**
Will color be applied in a gradient or blocked? How will you add interest to your quilt using color? Will you focus on value differences, or add interest with surprising colors?

**Improv technique**
Which improv technique will you use: ruler-cut or ruler-free? Will the improv choices solely come from color placement in a precision-pieced quilt? Will the improv choices come from sewing technique and contain organized color design? Or will you combine multiple improv techniques to get your desired results?

**Combined shapes**
What traditional quilt shapes will you include in your design? How often will these shapes occur? Will all shapes in the design be non-traditional quilt shapes?

**Construction**
Will you use a block-based design to eliminate complicated puzzling together of sections? Will your design be less formal and more organic? Will you incorporate or avoid partial or Y-seams?

**Areas of interest**
How will you capture the viewer's eye? What areas will draw the audience to the quilt? How will these areas be featured: with color, shape, repetition, balance? How will you include areas of rest or negative space?

"By smashing together your favorite quilt shapes ... and applying color thoughtfully, you can create your own voice."

# Project 9: Medallion Quilt

If you've made it this far, then you will have developed and polished some important skills needed for improv quilting. However, being thrown in front of a blank design wall can still be intimidating. Now is the time to put together your favorite quilt shapes and techniques with a guided approach to an improv medallion quilt.

A medallion quilt is a traditional quilt style that can be converted into an exciting improv journey.

Please read through all the instructions for this project before starting. Here you will combine your improv skills using ruler-cut, ruler-free, or both techniques to create a medallion quilt built with a central motif surrounded by borders. Choose a color harmony or use your rainbow.

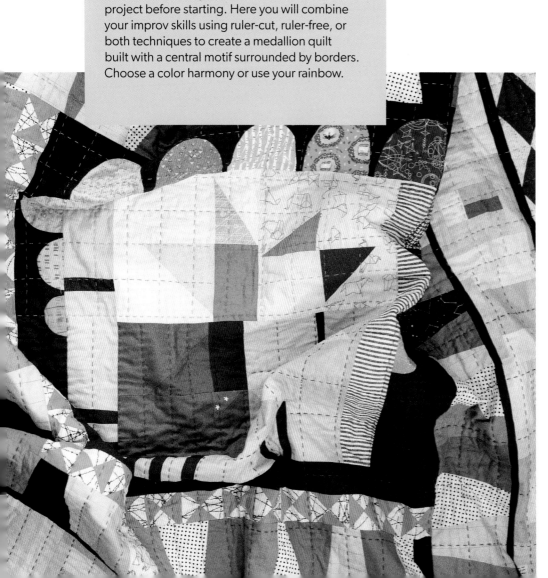

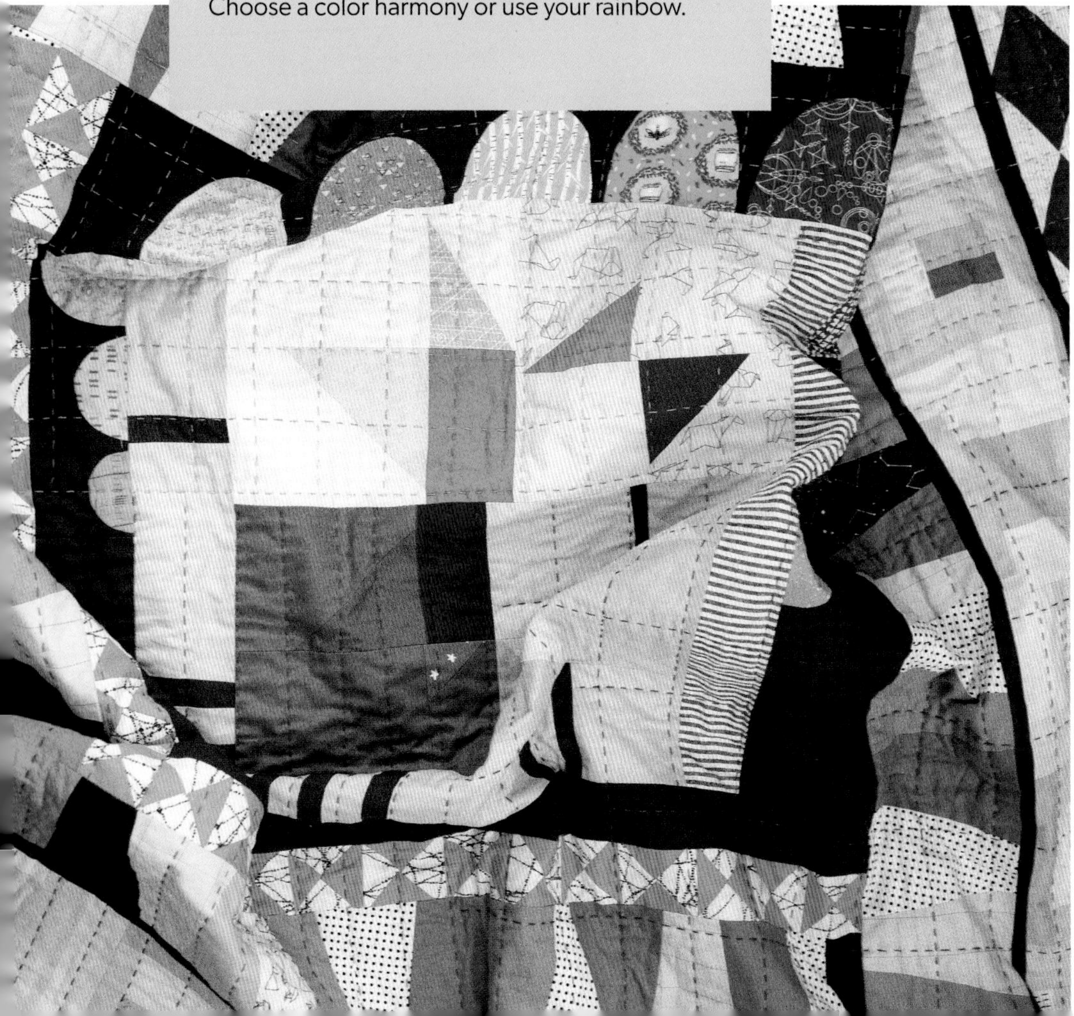

I have selected to use my rainbow colors for this project. Each border contains a different use of my rainbow. Including rainbow gradient, color blocking, value differences, or placement of a color that stands out.

The finished sample quilt is 65½ x 63½in (166 x 161cm).

Aim for a finished quilt size around 55 x 55in (140 x 140cm) to 68 x 70in 173 x 178cm).

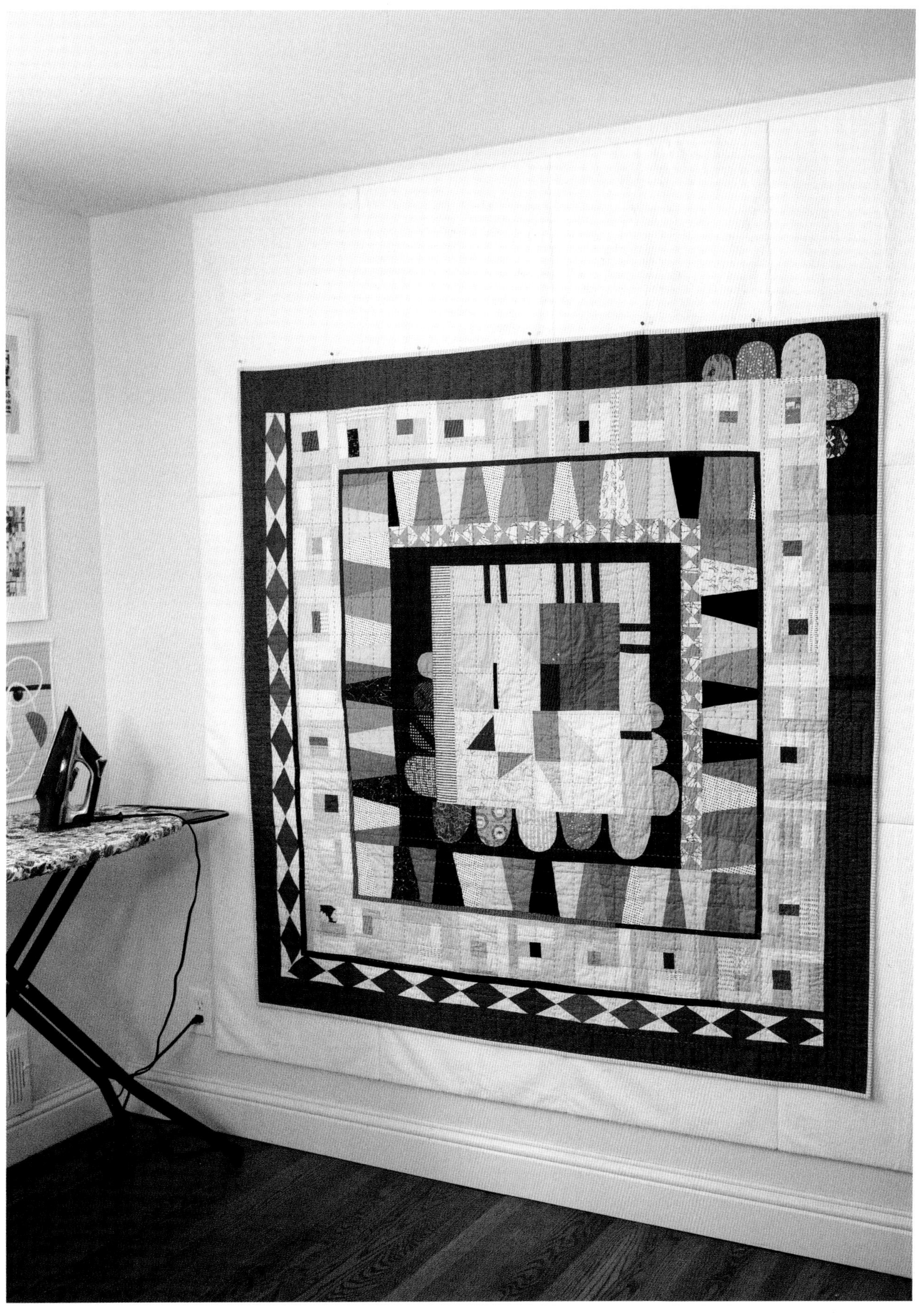

## Make a list

Make a list of different quilt blocks, shapes, or units that you may want to incorporate into your design.

Some examples of what to include on your list are:

- Diamonds
- Flying Geese
- Hourglass
- HRTs
- HSTs
- Log Cabin
- Negative space
- Pinwheel
- Pluses/X-shapes
- Quarter circles
- Scallops
- Squares
- Stars
- Stripes
- Triangles
- Wedges

## Create the center

Make a center motif by selecting a favorite quilt block and sewing it using an improv technique. The center does not need to be symmetrical or square.

A good size for a center block is between 12in (30cm) and 18in (46cm).

## Play

After assembling your center motif it is now time to play. Randomly select from the list of quilt shapes and choose how many sides to apply this to: one to four. Build each border and use fillers as needed. Working from the center motif out, continue to select from the list and choose the number of sides to apply the border to.

Try to add 5–7 borders, each approximately 2–5in (5–13cm) wide.

## TIPS

- Use an orphan block for the center motif.
- Choose quilt shapes from a hat to get a more random selection.
- Roll a die to determine the number of sides the border will be applied to.
- The border selected does not need to be symmetrical.
- Insert interesting or out-of-place colors throughout the borders.
- Tie back to the center motif by repeating shapes or fabrics that appear in the center.
- Make borders different widths to add interest.

## Finishing the quilt

See notes on quilt finishing, pages 116–122.

The sample quilt is quilted by hand with multiple grid and straight-line designs. The binding is sewn by hand.

# Project 10: Combined Skills

You should be confident in working with improv techniques after practicing with the previous projects.

**From projects 1 and 2:** Your takeaway was how to choose and distribute colors that you enjoy working with (and even some you don't like).

**From projects 3 and 4:** You learned how to develop your improv ruler-cut skills, first using a traditional block, and then more freeform.

**From project 4:** You also worked out how to look at shapes that were not in a block format to create groups that could be pieced together without— or with minimal use of—partial seams.

**From projects 5 and 6:** Ruler-free improv allowed for a softer approach to piecing an improv quilt. Don't forget the mirrored contour!

**From projects 7 and 8:** You mastered complicated piecing of curves, wedges, and arcs.

**From project 8:** You also discovered how to puzzle together sections of your quilt to limit the need for partial seams by using filler pieces.

**From project 9:** By building a medallion quilt you learned how to create an organized composition of your favorite quilt shapes and colors.

Please read through all the instructions for this project before starting. You will practice prioritizing elements in a quilt composition to create a balanced design.

The finished sample quilt size is 59 x 65in (150 x 165cm).

Aim for a finished quilt size approximately 50 x 55in (127 x 140cm) to 65 x 70in (165 x 178cm).

# Planning

Now is the time to approach a blank design wall and conquer it!

However, this does not mean having zero plans. Create a menu of your preferences to reference while designing your quilt. Remember to ask yourself questions about the design, such as the ones in the list below.

**Design preference menu**

- What color harmony will I choose?
- Will I add colors that are not included in my chosen harmony, or colors I am not drawn to in order to create interest?
- What improv technique will I choose: ruler-cut or ruler-free? Will I use a combination of techniques?
- Do I want all my seams to be horizontal and vertical, or are angled or curved seams okay too?
- Will I use prints, solids, or a combination of fabric types? Will I include a background fabric?
- Is there balance in piece sizes? Are there areas or color sections that need larger or smaller pieces added?
- Is there balance in value? Does each light area or dark area have an opposite light or dark area to balance the overall composition?
- Is there balance in repeating shapes? Design happens best in threes: intentionally add design elements to your quilt three times.
- Where do I need filler pieces? Will I add intentional filler pieces for interest?

## Assemble—quilt top

After answering some of the design questions, begin by making an initial fabric pull. Create your own coloring sheet for color placement if necessary. Your quilt shapes do not need to be identified on your color-placement sketch. Reference the list of shapes from project 9, page 106, to use in this project.

Start sewing. Make a single unit or a group of quilt shapes and place them on your design wall. Reference your design preference menu (see opposite) to remind yourself where your design will lead. Don't be afraid to move around different sections of the quilt on the design wall as you build your quilt.

Most importantly, have fun!

The sample quilt uses some of my favorite elements from the previous projects. From project 1, I am using a traditional Nine-Patch block. I chose to use my rainbow colors from project 2. My selected improv technique is ruler-free cutting. As in project 6, I am using larger piecing; this balances some of the more detailed piecing. From project 8, I am using wonky stars to add interest, repeated in three areas of the quilt.

## Finishing the quilt

See notes on quilt finishing, pages 116–122.

The sample quilt is quilted on a domestic machine with an edge-to-edge, walking-foot design. It is hand bound.

# 6 Finishing your quilt

"Hand quilting has long been an art practice."

After finishing the design and construction of a quilt top, your project is not yet complete. There are many factors to consider when it comes to finishing a quilt. In fact, finishing probably deserves its own book and not just a single chapter.

The choices you have when it comes to finishing your quilt start with basting and end with the final flourish of a label for your quilt. The opportunities you take when you quilt and bind will add an additional layer of depth to your quilt design.

Of course, there is more than one way to finish a quilt. This chapter will touch on several options for each step after your quilt top is complete. I will summarize some of my favorite finishing options. Choose your favorite methods and enjoy the process!

# BASTING

Basting (also known as tacking) is used to make a quilt sandwich with a quilt backing, batting, and quilt top. The three most common types of basting are pin basting, thread basting, and spray basting.

Before beginning basting, cut your backing fabric and batting approximately 6–8in (15–20cm) larger than your quilt top.

**Pin basting**
Spread the quilt back face down on a large flat surface. Place the batting layer on top of the quilt back. Add the quilt top face up on top of the batting. Flatten all layers before pinning. Tape edges to keep taut if necessary. Using safety pins, begin pinning at the center of the quilt. Pin through all layers and work towards the edges of the quilt, adding pins every 4–6in (10–15cm). Remove the safety pins as you approach them during quilting.

**Thread basting**
Layer your quilt sandwich on a large, flat surface as you would for pin basting. Beginning in the center of the quilt, stitch using 2–3in (5–7.5cm) long stitches in a thread of a contrasting color to your quilt top and your chosen quilting thread (as shown below left). Work your way from the center to the edges until the quilt sandwich is secure. Remove basting threads after quilting is complete.

**Spray basting**
Use a temporary fabric adhesive aerosol for spray basting. Place your batting on a large, flat surface and place the quilt back face up on top of the batting. Turn back half of the backing to reveal the batting underneath and work from the center of the quilt out. Following the instructions on the product, spray all the way across the quilt in a 6–8in (15–20cm) section. Lay the backing back on the batting where the adhesive is and smooth to flatten. Repeat spraying and smoothing until all the backing is attached.

Flip the batting and backing over and lay the quilt top right side up on top of the exposed batting. Turn back half of the quilt top to reveal the batting underneath and work from the center of the quilt outward, again, working across the quilt in 6–8in (15–20cm) sections. Lay the quilt top back on the batting where the adhesive is and smooth to flatten. Repeat spraying and smoothing until all the quilt top is attached. Some spray adhesives require a heat set. Gently press with a hot iron using the manufacturer's recommended temperature setting.

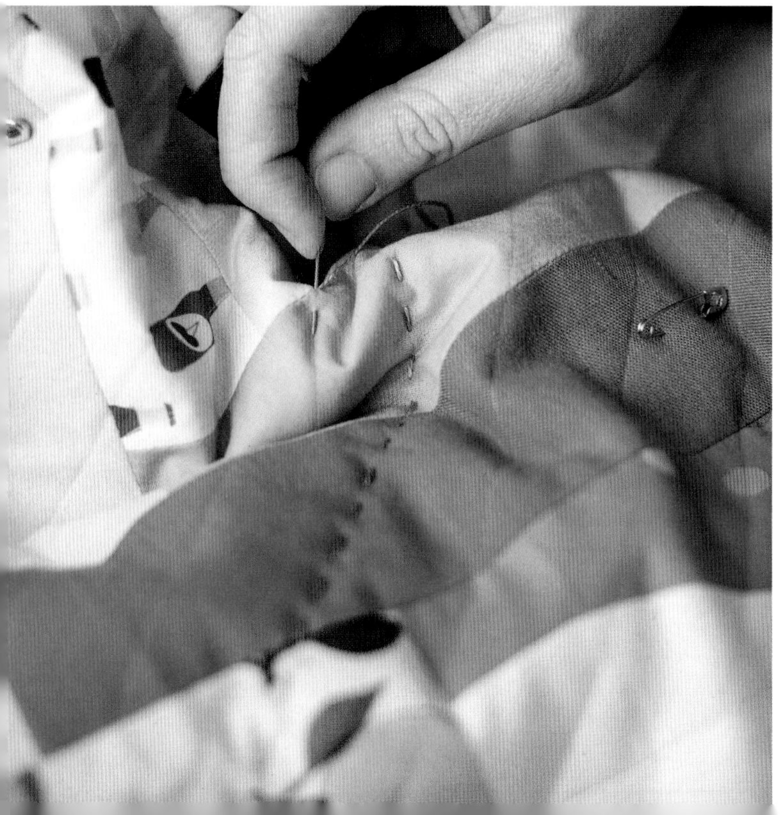

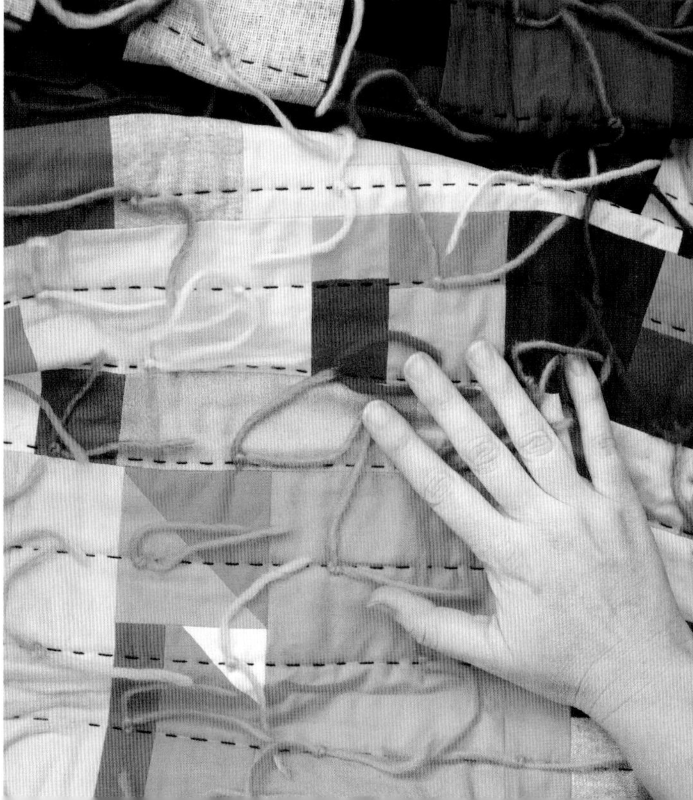

# QUILTING

There are many ways to attach the three layers of your quilt sandwich together. They include, but are not limited to, longarm quilting, domestic machine quilting, hand quilting, hand tying, or any combination.

**Longarm quilting**
You may choose to hire a quilting service like a longarm quilter. Longarm quilters offer a variety of services that may include computerized pantographs, free-motion quilting, and even custom quilting options. A longarm quilter may even offer basting services if you desire to do your own quilting and hire out the basting. Check with any services you hire for specific instructions on sizing the backing and batting.

**Domestic machine quilting**
Your domestic sewing machine is a powerful tool. You can use a darning foot and do free-motion quilting or a walking foot or dual-feed foot for curved or straight-line quilting. Don't be afraid to experiment with different thread weights and types. Larger numbers like a 100-weight silk or polyester will be the thinnest and will add crinkle to your finished project but the quilting lines will not be very visible. Cotton thread of 40- or 50-weight is the most common to use in a domestic machine for quilting. Heavier threads like a 28-weight will add more visibility to your quilting lines.

**Hand quilting**
Hand quilting has long been an art practice. If you are like me and don't have the patience or skill to stitch nearly invisible stitches with a nearly invisible needle, you may be interested in big-stitch quilting (shown on the far left). Using a size 12, 8, or 5 thread, you can add a lot of interest and texture to your quilt. I prefer to use a size 3–5 crewel needle paired with size 8 perle cotton thread.

**Quilt tying**
Tied quilts (as shown on the left) are a tried-and-true classic way of finishing a quilt. The best option is to use wool thread or yarn because it will naturally felt itself and become more secure with every wash. Cut long lengths of yarn and stitch across your quilt before clipping for individual ties or cut shorter lengths and stitch each tie individually for more color variation.

# BINDING

Binding or edge finishing also has several popular options. Self-binding, standard binding or bias binding attached by machine or hand, and facing can all be done in several widths.

### Self-binding

A self-bound quilt uses the backing fabric that is already part of the quilt sandwich as the binding. After quilting, cut the batting to the exact size of the quilt top. Trim the backing fabric 1in (2.5cm) larger than the quilt top and batting. Fold the backing fabric towards the quilt top to meet the edges together. Fold the backing fabric over the quilt top to conceal the edge of the quilt and the raw edge of the backing. At the corners, fold into a 45-degree angle to create a mitered corner. Secure the self-binding with clips or pins. Stitch to the face of the quilt by machine or hand.

### Standard and bias binding

Standard or bias binding is attached the same way but is cut either with the grain or at a 45-degree angle to the grain. Cut strips your preferred width—I like 2½in (6.5cm)—and sew them end-to-end. Press in half lengthwise. Matching the raw edges of the binding to the raw edge of the quilt, sew on by machine with a ¼in (5mm) seam allowance.

For hand-finished binding I attach the binding to the front/quilt top side. For machine-finished binding, I attach the binding to the back of the quilt first. At the corners, stop stitching ¼in (5mm) from the edge and secure with a backstitch. Fold the binding at a 45-degree angle away from the quilt, then fold the binding back over itself to align the binding and quilt edges. Begin stitching ¼in (5mm) from the edge, and secure with backstitching. This creates a mitered corner.

After the binding is secured around the entire perimeter of the quilt, fold the binding over and stitch down by machine or by hand.

Left: hand binding.

Below: an example of a faced quilt.

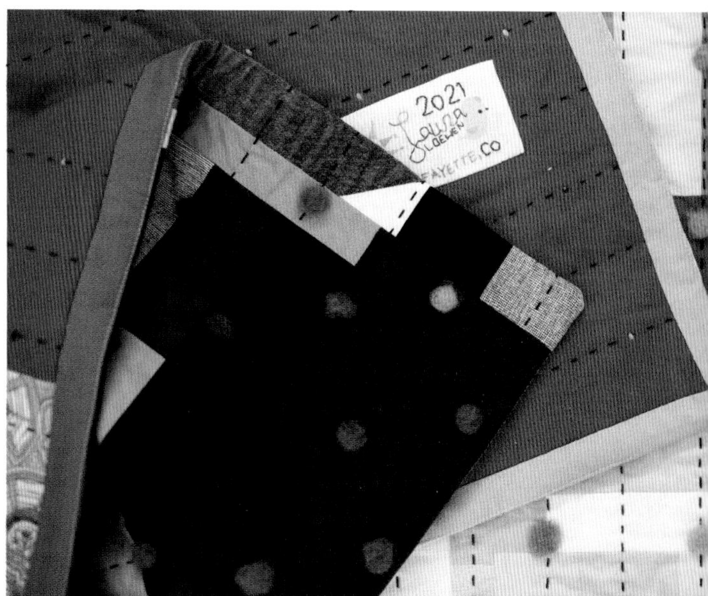

### Facing

Cut strips your preferred width: I like 2½in (6.5cm). Sew the strips together, if necessary, to create two strips the width of your quilt and two strips 3in (7.5cm) longer than the length of your quilt. Fold and press the strip for the quilt top lengthwise. Align the raw edges with the top edge of the quilt. Sew with a ¼in (5mm) seam allowance to the quilt front. Press the strip away from the quilt. Top-stitch on the strip along the edge of the quilt. Press the strip to the back side of the quilt. Pin or clip in place. Repeat for the bottom facing strip.

For side strips (3in/7.5cm longer than length of quilt), align the center of the strip edge with the center of the side edge of the quilt. Sew with a ¼in (5mm) seam allowance to the quilt front. Press the strip away from the quilt. Top-stitch on the strip along the edge of the quilt. Repeat for the other side facing strip. Manipulate the excess fabric at the corners to fold under any unfinished edges. Trim shorter if necessary. Pin or clip in place. Hand stitch the facing strips to the quilt backing along the folded edge of the strips.

This quilt is finished with domestic machine and hand quilting, and standard hand binding.

# LABELS

Don't forget to label your quilts! You can create a simple label using a scrap of fabric and a fineliner pen. Fold under the raw edges and hand stitch your label on the back of your quilt.

Alternatively, you can stitch your label on by machine. If you match your bobbin thread to your quilting thread color, it will hardly be noticeable. Of course, your label can be as decorative or as detailed as you want it to be. Embroider, paint, stamp, fussy cut, or even print a label of your choosing.

Common things to include on a quilt label are the maker's name, quilter's name, quilt name, year completed, location completed, recipient's name, occasion for gift, occasion for making quilt, and/or pattern name. You can include or leave off whatever you'd like.

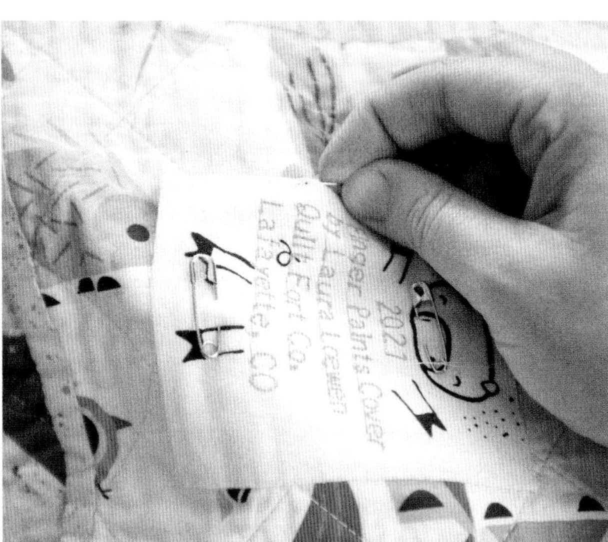

# Coloring sheets

Photocopy the relevant coloring sheet before you work on each project. Refer to the project instructions and look back to Chapter 1: Color play (pages 20–27) for more on choosing the color harmonies for your quilts.

## Project 1: Irish Chain, pages 28–33

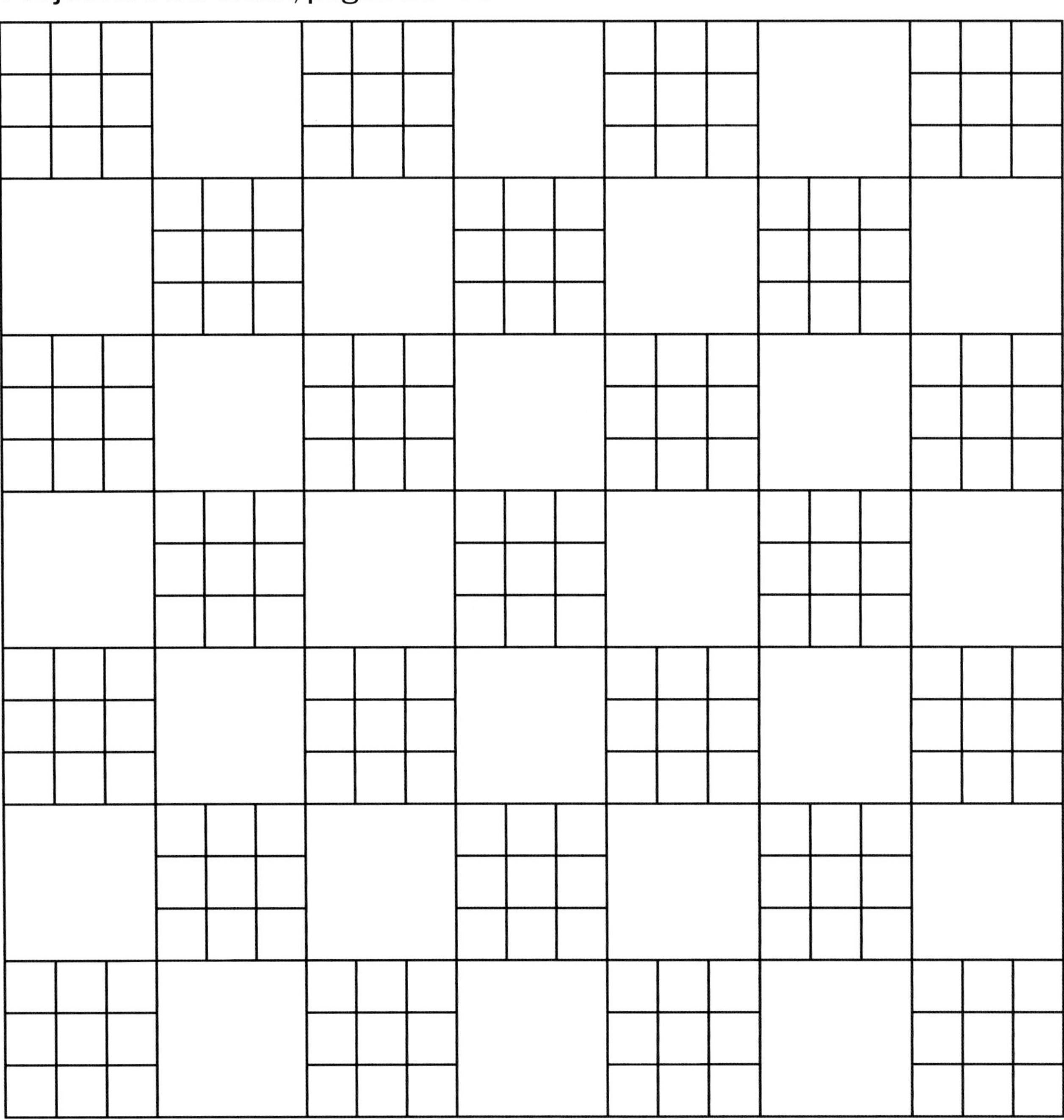

These templates are also available to download free from the Bookmarked Hub: www.bookmarkedhub.com. Search for this book by title or ISBN: the files can be found under 'Book Extras'. Membership of the Bookmarked online community is free.

## Project 3: Sawtooth Star, pages 48–55

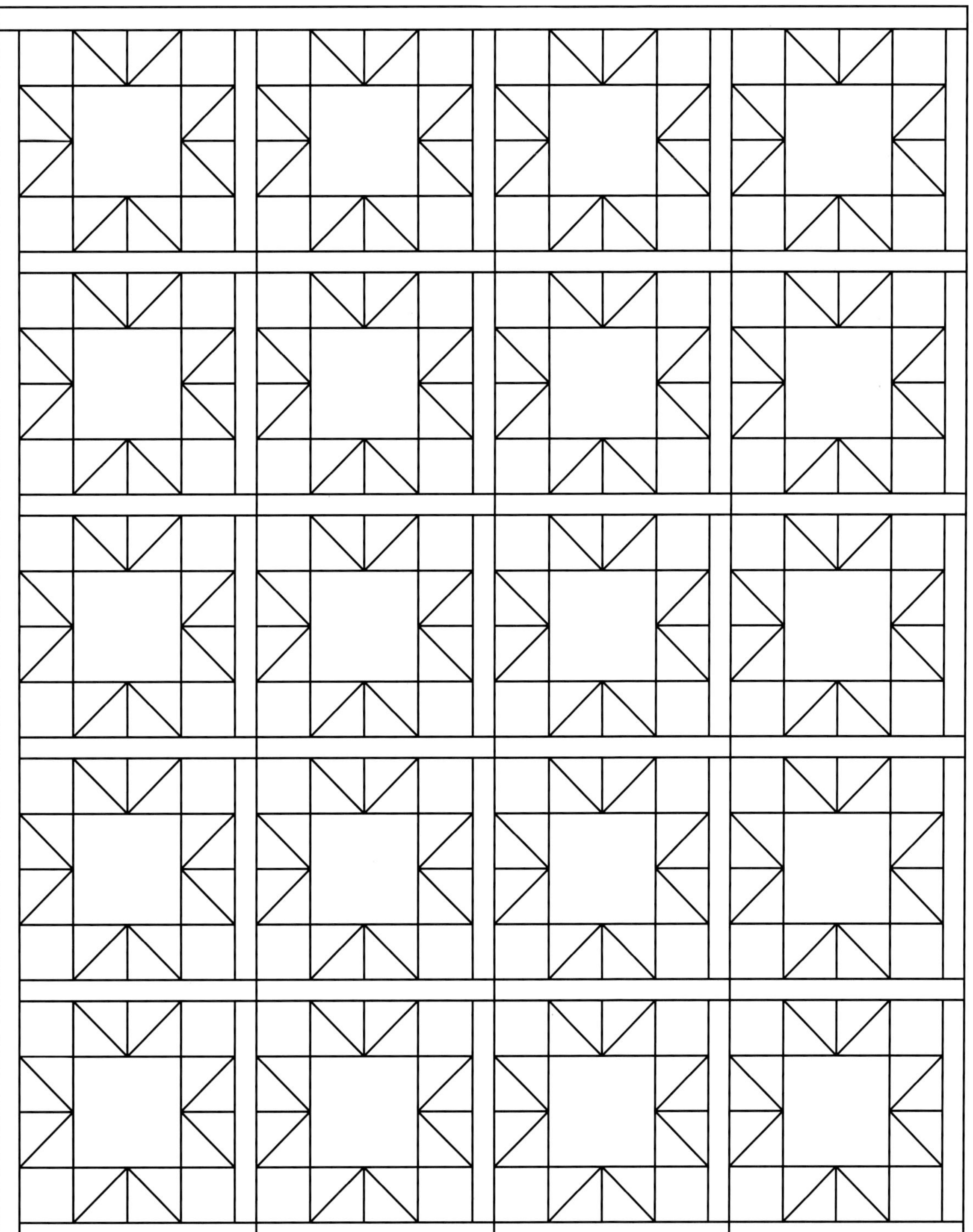

# Project 5: Squash Blossom, pages 68–75

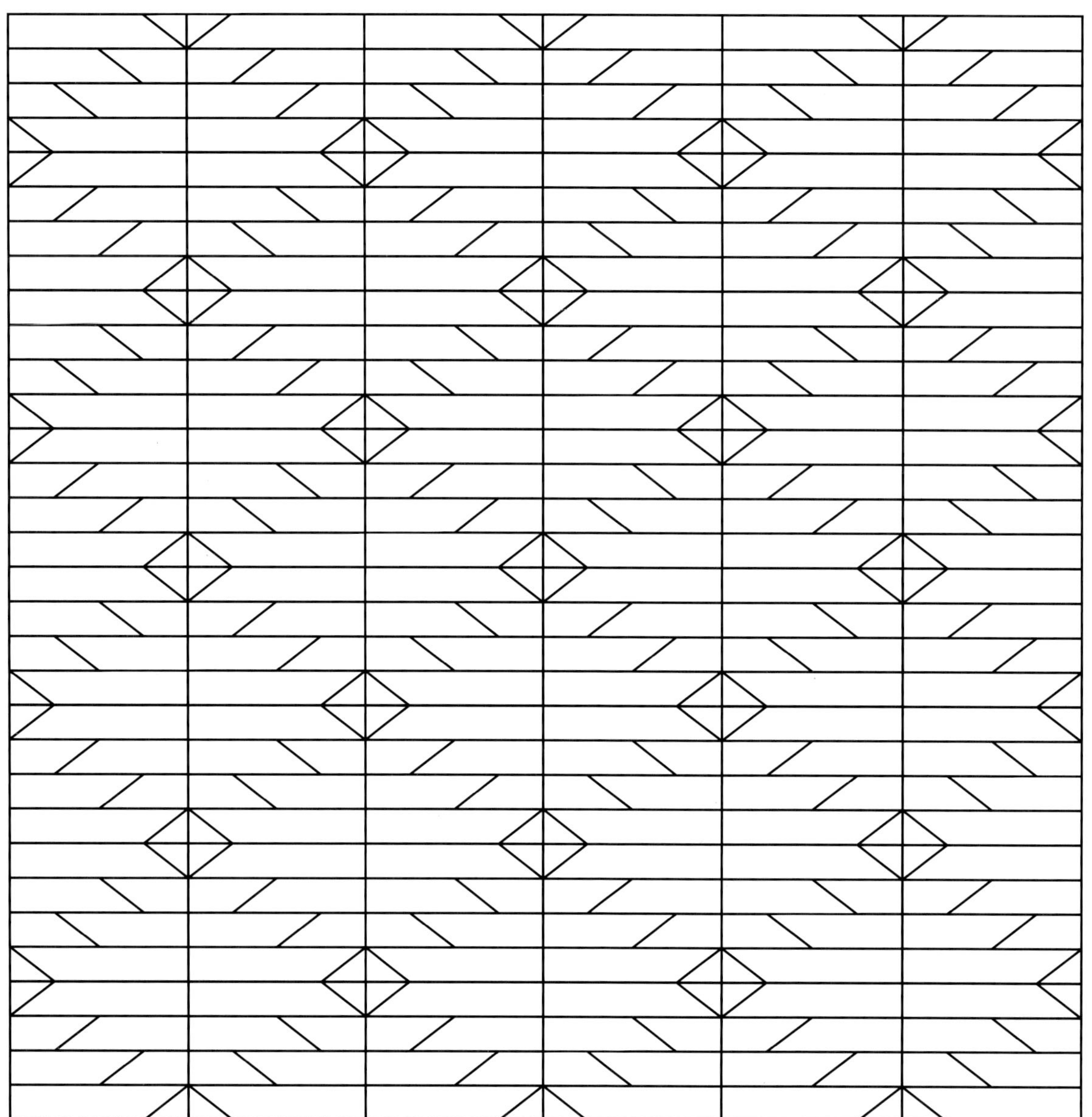

## Project 7: Wagon Wheel, pages 86–91

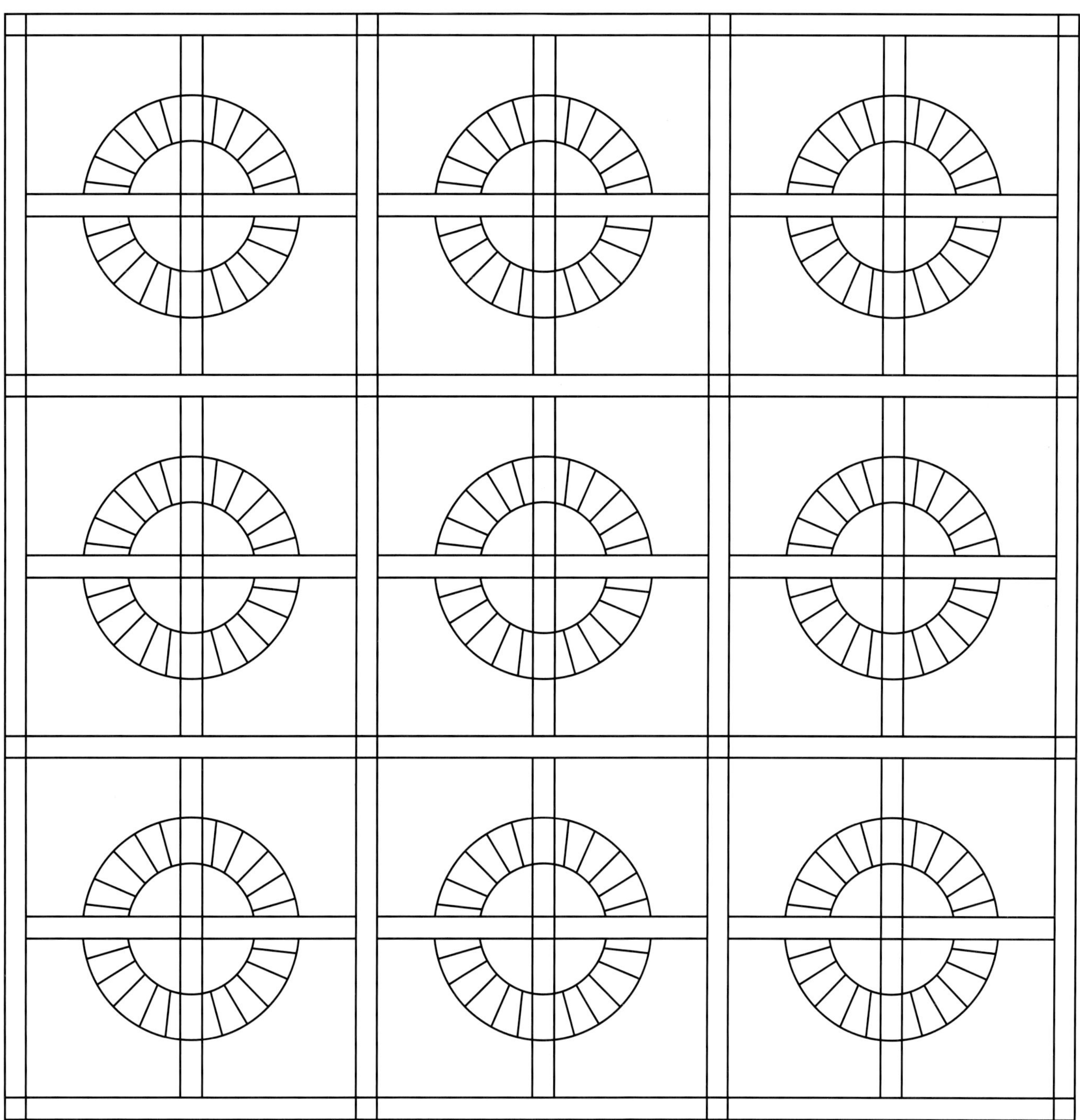

# Index